You're Over Thinking It

FIND LIFELONG LOVE BY BEING YOUR TRUE SELF

Sabrina Alexis Bendory

AMARYLLIS

AMARYLLIS
An imprint of Manjul Publishing House Pvt. Ltd.
• C-16, Sector 3, Noida, Uttar Pradesh 201301, India
Website: www.manjulindia.com
Registered Office:
• 2nd Floor, Usha Preet Complex,
42, Malviya Nagar, Bhopal 462 003 - India
Distribution Centres
Ahmedabad, Bengaluru, Chennai, Hyderabad,
Kochi, Kolkata, Mumbai, Noida, Pune

You're Overthinking It: Find Lifelong Love By Being Your True Self
by Sabrina Alexis Bendory

This edition first published in India in 2025

ISBN 978-93-5543-575-0

Printed and bound in India by Replika Press Pvt. Ltd.

Table of Contents

Introduction

If you're anything like how I used to be, then love and relationships haven't exactly come easy to you.

You may have spent the better part of your adult life envisioning and dreaming up what your perfect relationship would look like and have been left jaded and blindsided time and time again when things took a sudden and unexpected turn.

You found out the guy who you thought was your soulmate fell in love with another woman through a Facebook post (yup, happened to me). You started dating an incredible guy, the chemistry was palpable, the conversation flowed effortlessly, your values aligned...and just when you started thinking this was *it*, he ghosts you. He's gone with no explanation and you feel like you've been knocked sideways. Or maybe you desperately want to get back together with your ex boyfriend. You know you're perfect together, you know this could work, you know this *will* work, but he doesn't feel the same and wants no part of it and you just can't let go. Or maybe you met an amazing guy and everything is great...but he won't call you his girlfriend. He doesn't like labels, he wants to keep things as they are, he just has so much going on with work. He wants you, but not in the way you want him to. Maybe all of your relationships seem to go this way and you're at the point where you just expect things to fall apart before they even really begin. Or maybe you've been single for what feels like forever and you just don't get it. Why can't you find love? Why is it so hard?

Maybe you just can't seem to get it right. Maybe you sometimes feel like there is some sort of conspiracy against you. Maybe you're afraid of ending up alone.

I feel you and I hear you because I *was* you.

And my quest to understand and get a handle on my love life turned into a really successful career. What felt like an unsolvable riddle became so clear to me and I've spent the last 13 years sharing my knowledge and helping countless women all over the world find lasting love. And by the time you finish this book, you will be well on your way.

This is not a book full of tricks and gimmicks. This book will reveal the truth about relationships and the truth about yourself. You will learn exactly why love has been so evasive for you and what it takes to attract love that lasts.

You will *finally* break free of the cycle of endlessly analyzing and stressing over your relationships. You will arrive at a beautiful land called clarity where you will understand what went wrong in the past and what you can do today to become the woman you've always wanted to be and get the relationship you've always wanted.

I was where you are, I wanted what you want. I desperately just wanted to understand. I wanted to find lasting love. I wanted to learn how to love myself. I wanted to feel empowered and sure of myself. I wanted to stop all the stressing and *overthinking* and just get what I wanted out of life.

And I did. And I've helped many, many people just like you and I promise, you will get there!

So, Who Am I & Why Should You Listen To Me?

In short, I am you.

For the last decade plus, I've essentially been writing for my younger self. I've been writing everything I wish I would have known.

It started with a website, and then there was an email list...and e-books...and audio courses...and then a YouTube channel...and all the social media. No matter what platform, millions of women all around the world have found wisdom, insight, empowerment, and lasting love from following my advice.

I have always believed that everything happens for a reason. Call me a doe-eyed optimist, but that is one of my convictions that has never really wavered. When I was 17, I met a boy who made my heart beat a little differently from the rest. He just had a certain something that I was never able to find again. The relationship wasn't serious, but it was *significant*. I was crazy about him. And I just remember feeling OK whenever I talked to him. I just felt *right*, like this was how things were supposed to be. I can't quite explain it; it was just this feeling of quiet calm. The relationship failed and he ended up being my first major heartbreak. I wanted something serious, he wanted to be a freshman in college and take nothing seriously—save for an intense game of beer pong. I was crushed. I analyzed and replayed the relationship on loop for months. That was probably the start of my quest to understand men...the never-ending quest that turned into a career! But all's well that ends well, we are actually now married with three kids!

Experience is the greatest teacher, and my relationship experiences have given me a wealth of invaluable knowledge. My entire life has been consumed by relationships. I'm *in* a relationship, but I also spend most of my time reading about relationships, talking to people about their relationships, writing about relationships, and observing relationships. It's a fascinating topic that I'll never get bored with because there is always so much more to learn. And that's the sad part, actually. It's such an important topic, but so few people get the education they need to have successful, happy relationships.

Rejection can be a crushing, gutting experience, and even though there is much greater pain in the world, and even though I certainly am not the only girl to have had her heart broken, at the time it truly felt like no one on the entire planet could possibly fathom what I was going through.

When I created A New Mode, I really aimed to create a place that would foster that feeling of sisterhood, a place where women could find understanding and answers. I am still stunned by the fact that women of all ages and from every corner of the world, write to me with the exact same questions, the exact same pain, and all they want are answers and understanding.

You're Overthinking It...

I have written a lot over the years, like *a lot*. I have so much material in the form of articles, newsletters, books, YouTube videos, and audio programs it literally took me two months to sort through it all. This book is a compilation of some of my best work. The content that hit the hardest made the strongest impression, and really got people thinking and talking.

The fact is, getting what you want in life isn't as out of reach as it may seem. It isn't an epic mountain to climb. You just need the right tools and to learn how to utilize them properly. You already have everything you need...I'm just here to teach you how to use it.

The problem usually starts in your own mind. It's the thoughts and stories we tell ourselves. And the good news is, you have complete control over your mind! And when you get a handle on your mindset, everything will change for you.

Here is where so many of us go wrong.

Most people just don't know what makes for a healthy relationship and what sets the foundation for a healthy relationship. It really starts with having a clear understanding of what a healthy relationship looks like. Most people don't have this because mainstream media only shows us dysfunctional relationships, since those are more fun to watch.

In terms of how to get to that strong place internally, it's really about getting your mind under control, learning to manage your thoughts and perspectives, and not feeding into thoughts that feel bad to you.

A lot of people create stories about themselves based on the things that happen. For example, your partner leaves you for someone else and you tell yourself, "It's because I'm unloveable and unworthy and every guy I truly care for will find someone better." This story becomes hardwired into your psyche and has an effect on your future relationships, even though it isn't a conscious thought.

You carry the pain into your next relationship and bring all that anxiety with you, which prevents you from being able to be present and form a connection. Then that relationship fails and you use that as further proof that you are unworthy, and on and on the cycle goes until you finally challenge those faulty beliefs that were wired into your brain.

Once we learn how to undo the stories we tell ourselves, and more importantly, once we get our thoughts and relationship anxiety under control, not only can we have the relationship we want, we can have anything we want in life.

You have so much more power over your life than you realize. In this book, I'll show you how to use it.

While my last book, *10 Things Every Woman Needs to Know About Men*, was all about understanding men and why they act the way they do, I wanted to create a resource that focused more on you and your experience of getting and being in a relationship. The tools I share will help you attract lasting love, but they will also help you foster a better, healthier relationship with yourself. You will learn how to increase your feelings of self-worth and self-esteem, and we've all heard that you can only find love from the outside when you feel it on the inside.

This book applies whether you're single or taken, whether you're a man or a woman. One key thing I've observed is that it takes the same skills to get a relationship as it does to be in a relationship—at least a happy, loving, mutually fulfilling relationship.

And it takes the same skills to be good at relationships as it does to be good at life. Everything is connected.

What I share in the book can help you in all areas of your life: career, parenthood, reducing anxiety, being healthier overall, and so much more. This book is about getting what you want in life and being the person you want to be.

While this book is a compilation of my previous work, there are also plenty of new insights, stories, and ideas. I really wanted to provide a thorough look at relationships from the inside out. I wanted to look at why so many relationships falter and what it takes to avoid that and get the amazing relationship you've always wanted—and how to do it by being your absolute true self. No pretense, no facade, no becoming something you're not.

I organized this book in a way to break it all down and make it crystal clear so you have no more questions, no more stress, no more *overthinking*, only clarity.

So let's dive in and look at exactly what you need to know to have the love (and life) you've always wanted.

CHAPTER 1

Choosing the Right Partner

"Women cannot complain about men anymore until they start getting better taste in them." —*Bill Maher*

All the relationship advice in the world won't make any difference if you're choosing the wrong partner. This is the step that often gets missed or overlooked. We hammer away, trying to pound the proverbial square peg into a round hole, then wonder what we're doing wrong, why we can't seem to make it fit, why we can't get the love we want. You can't turn a losing stock into a winning stock. You can't force someone to change and to want what you want. You can't convince someone to feel a certain way about you.

I spent way too long chasing after guys who wouldn't or couldn't give me what I wanted, and then I wondered what was wrong with *me* when it didn't get me lasting love! The problem was simple: I was choosing the wrong men. It sounds straightforward enough, but it's a very tricky thing. We fall for these people because it feels so right, because we're swept up in the passion, the chemistry, and the intoxicating aura of unavailability; we get sucked into the space that exists when someone is just beyond our reach and it makes us yearn for them. We convince ourselves that this is *it*, that they're the one and we just need to make them see it.

This is where the problems develop. This is where all the questions and tears and doubt and uncertainties and fears start to consume you. You mistake these feelings for true love because maybe you've never felt this way before, and you think it must be because this person is different and this relationship is meant to last.

This is just a glimpse into the confusion that ensues when you choose the wrong partner. If you're hung up on someone who can't commit or won't commit or who is mean to you or who is just a mean person in general, a person with baggage, a person with serious issues, a person who you think would be perfect "if only" they changed such and such, then you're setting yourself up to lose before you even begin, and you are blocking yourself from ever finding the love you want.

Where Healthy Relationships Begin

Before we talk about what to look for in a partner, it's important to look at how relationships begin. The start of a relationship can oftentimes color our lenses and sometimes lead us down a bad path and into a toxic relationship.

Here's a situation that may sound familiar to you. You meet someone, something clicks, and suddenly it feels like a force outside of you has taken over.

After this encounter you can't—for the life of you—get this guy out of your head. You try to think about other things but nothing works. You ruminate over every detail of your interaction with him—what he said, what you said, what his body language said. You think about the things you *wish* you had said.

You check your phone constantly to see if he called or texted. If he does, your stomach drops, your heart races, you want to leap off your seat and shout for joy. And then of course you need to figure out the exact right thing to say back to him, the perfect quip to show him that you're made for each other.

The high continues as you venture into a relationship, and it becomes even more intense. You never quite know where you stand with him. The uncertainty keeps you on your toes, constantly on alert for something that looks like a bad sign or an ominous foreshadowing. This emotional rollercoaster is as thrilling as it is exhausting. You're hooked. The worst possible thing that could happen is him leaving. It's a fear you can't quite shake no matter how promising the situation looks, a fear that drives everything you say and do.

Now another scenario.

You meet a guy, you think he's nice and all, you have a good conversation, and he gets your number. While you're pleased, you don't go into a tizzy over it. You may check his social media accounts, but only for a few minutes. You are happy to hear from him if he calls or texts, but you don't notice the hours that pass in between your interactions. You go out a few times, not expecting much, but soon enough your interest and attraction begin to grow. Things feel calm, there's no drama, no heart palpitations... and it feels really nice.

Which relationship do you think has a stronger chance of survival?

Instinctively, you would say the second one. In real life, you would fall for the first. That's because the first scenario illustrates everything we've ever been told about love.

In movies and romance novels, love is this grand, all-consuming force that takes you over in the most dramatic of ways. There are huge obstacles to overcome, but it's OK because love conquers all! I mean, would any of us have cared for "The Notebook" if Ali and Noah were of the same social status, went on a few lukewarm dates, then got to know each other and developed a deepening connection over time? Don't think so.

Unhealthy Relationships Start With A Pull

Relationships that start from a place of pure, unadulterated passion can seldom survive unless they have some substance and depth of connection to stand on. Explosive chemistry isn't what creates a lasting, healthy relationship. It can lead to great sex and feelings of euphoria, and you may come to understand why they say love is a drug, but no matter how intense and all consuming, that sort of thing is seldom sustainable long term.

When you feel a strong and sudden pull towards someone else, the kind that causes you to turn him from mere mortal to deity-like being, something else is at play, something that isn't exactly what you would call romantic. There are a few good reasons why we might become inexplicably drawn to someone who isn't good for us.

Imago Theory

This theory, developed by clinical pastoral counselor Harville Hendrix, PhD, posits that the pull we feel towards another person is guided by our unconscious desire to rectify some issue from our past. Imago is Latin for image, and the theory essentially states that we unconsciously seek partners who reflect the image of our primary caregivers so that we can try to heal lingering wounds inflicted by them by working through issues with someone in their image. These relationships present the opportunity to heal ourselves and become whole again, but they also pose the risk of continuing to pour salt into open wounds.

How it pans out is something like this: If your parents always made you feel like you weren't good enough, you may seek out guys who make you feel like you're not good enough, then try to win them over in an attempt to rectify those painful feelings from your past.

If your father was very critical, you may find yourself drawn to a man who is very critical, trying to win his love and approval in order to heal from the hurt of your father's rejection. These decisions aren't conscious, they happen very deep beneath the surface in areas we can't easily access. When we meet someone, we immediately sense everything about him, especially the way he makes us feel (again, this happens unconsciously).

On a conscious level, you may assess the things he says, but on an unconscious level, you're looking at his body language, his tone, the way he phrases things, how much eye contact he makes, his whole demeanor. If your unconscious finds something familiar in that person, something that reminds you of an unresolved hurt from the past, it will light up and push you towards that person.

You may also unconsciously seek out partners who have some quality that is underdeveloped in you. For example, if you're a Type A workaholic and always wished you could ease up, you may be drawn to a laid-back partner who isn't so driven. Or maybe you just feel all over the place, like your life is unsettled, and you're drawn to someone stable who seems to have it all together.

Maybe this sounds a little too New Age-y to you, or maybe it doesn't describe your situation at all, but it's a powerful concept and it has gained a lot of praise and recognition in the field of psychology so it's worth considering.

Infatuation

Being infatuated sounds like a grand, romantic thing, but it can actually be quite problematic. The problem with infatuation is it isn't based on anything real. Infatuation causes you to fall in love with an image rather than an actual person. It causes you to put someone on a pedestal and overlook his flaws. Since he's so "perfect," you become afraid to be yourself—I mean, how could your true self *ever* compete with perfection?

You don't want to say the wrong thing and scare him off, so you aren't genuine in your interactions. You rely on his approval so desperately that you also become a bit needy. You may not act needy, but it's something that lurks beneath the surface and he will pick up on it...people always do. You lose your sense of worth because it becomes so wrapped up in how someone feels about you..

The biggest sign you're infatuated is not being able to find a single flaw in the other person. Infatuation usually happens because you have a void in your life that he fills. You don't feel good enough about yourself and this supreme being shows interest in you, making you feel desirable and worthy, and so you cling to him for more of that feeling.

When you're infatuated, the object of your desire usually comes to represent something to you. Maybe this person is extremely attractive, and throughout your life the attractive people never wanted you and you internalized the idea that if someone really hot wants you, then that makes you worthy (middle school trauma will mess you up like this!). So you become obsessed with this person, you feel like you *need* them and if it doesn't work out you will be plunged to the depths of despair with no way out...but really you don't need them, you need to heal that old wound within yourself. You're seeing this person as the answer to a problem only you can solve by diving in there and doing that inner work.

The inner work is scary. No one wants to go into the dark depths of their trauma. There is almost a fear that you'll get lost in the depths and won't find your way out. It's much easier to think that all you need to do is get this amazing person to love you...once they do, you will be all whole and healed.

Healthy Relationships Build Slowly

Healthy relationships usually begin with mutual interest and attraction that grows over time. This is the complete opposite of unhealthy relationships, which usually start out with a grand light show that quickly simmers into ash. A relationship psychologist once told me: The right relationship feels like home, not Hollywood. If you can internalize this, it will change the way you date forever.

The most important trait to develop is objectivity. No one really talks about that because it's not so sexy, but if you want to find lasting love and prevent yourself from getting hurt, you'll need to learn how to use your head a little more than your heart, at least in the beginning. Your heart can lead you into all kinds of bad places. Your heart is the one that tells you it's a great idea to go for the bad boy who's just *so* dreamy, even when he's out on parole and struggling with addictions, or has told you he won't ever be in a committed relationship. Your heart convinces you that the heart wants what the heart wants, and who are you to deny your heart? Your heart doesn't operate according to reason or rationality. It makes you do things that you later look back on and wonder, *what was I thinking?* But you *weren't* thinking. That's not what the heart does. OK, I know I'm being mean to the heart. It does have its benefits, but that comes later. In the beginning of a relationship, it's best to remain as objective as possible and try to keep your emotions mostly contained.

The best way to do this is to try to go slowly. Ease into the relationship instead of diving in head first. This will create an environment for you to allow your level of interest and attraction to grow steadily over time, rather than flooding you all at once in a big emotional tsunami.

If you spend all your time with him, you risk overlooking critical information about who he really is and if the relationship is built to last. Just because two people feel strongly for each other it doesn't always mean they can be together.

It is imperative to have a foundation of compatibility, shared goals and interests, and common values. Some things simply can't be negotiated. Before you emotionally invest, it is wise to determine if you are *fundamentally compatible*. And the best way to do this is to go slowly. I don't necessarily mean physically, I mean emotionally.

When you first meet someone, you want to spend every minute of every day with him. You talk for hours and hours on the phone, text all day, you can't get enough. The obvious reason this is problematic is because you may end up relying too heavily on the relationship for your happiness, but also, you don't get a break from the emotional excitement and stimulation of it all. Then, if you realize this guy may not be right for you, you'll be in too deep to get yourself out of the situation. You'll instead rely on some cliché like "love conquers all" to justify staying with him.

I am not saying to stay away from guys you feel a strong immediate attraction to and only date guys you're only "meh" about. I think you should date both kinds of guys—the infatuation guy could turn out to be a loser and the "meh" guy could turn out to be the love of your life. I've seen it happen countless times!

Either way, you have to date smart. This will come more naturally with "meh" than it will with the object of your infatuation.

If you just met or just started seeing someone, I strongly advise that you try to limit how much time you spend with him early on. Try to not go on more than two dates a week or engage in marathon texting sessions that go all day. When you do this, you never get a break from the emotional high and you don't get a chance to come back down and recalibrate.

So many girls make the mistake of getting caught up in how the guy feels about them rather than focusing on how *they* feel about *him*.

You can avoid falling into this trap by doing regular reality checks. Make sure you see him and the situation clearly. The best way to do this is to make sure you can recognize his flaws. The way you know you're infatuated is if you see no flaws. *Everyone* has flaws.

Why It Matters

When you get in over your head, you may convince yourself that something like him wanting to live only in the country and you wanting to live only in the city is not such a big deal. Someone who maintains a more objective perspective would acknowledge that she would be miserable living in the country, and since this guy wouldn't choose to live anywhere else, she would leave him.

I've seen (and personally experienced) many situations where a couple breaks up after a long period of time because of some issue that was apparent right from the beginning—they're of different religions, want to live in different states, one person doesn't want kids. In every one of these situations, the couple believed that things would magically just work out. Imagine how much time and effort they would have saved and how much heartbreak they would have avoided had they been dating with their heads instead of their hearts from the beginning.

Masculine & Feminine Energy

Before we go further, I want to address an important point.

Throughout this book I describe the ways men and women act in relationships and I mostly speak to women who date men. However, the concepts are universally applicable and don't only apply to specific genders in specific relationships.

Within all of us there exists a balance of masculine and feminine energy. So when I say "men" I mostly mean "masculine energy." For example, later in the book I talk about the fact that when a man is feeling emotionally off balance he will often want to retreat and work on it on his own—this also happens to be the way I cope when I'm stressed. The typical "feminine" reaction is to seek out those you are closest to and lean on them for support. So in this regard, I operate from a more masculine energy (and my husband actually seeks out others for support, so he is more tapped into his feminine energy in that respect).

All of us have different proportions of the masculine and feminine—there are men who may have a higher degree of "feminine" energy and vice versa.

In any sort of couple, you rarely see two people with the same energy levels—there is usually a balance between the two, a yin and yang effect.

Masculine energy is often focused and goal-oriented (this makes sense from an evolutionary standpoint when men had to go out and hunt and being distracted could mean being eaten by a lion). When a man is plugged into that masculine energy, nothing exists outside of the goal at hand. His head isn't in the relationship, he's not thinking about the errands he needs to run, nothing exists outside of the goal at hand.

Masculine energy has a harder time shifting gears and multitasking. Again, for the same reasons.

Feminine energy is better able to flow and handle multiple things at the same time. Feminine energy has the ability to be at work, and performing the tasks perfectly, while simultaneously texting with her partner, ordering the groceries online, taking care of the bills etc.

Masculine energy is giving and being a provider. And if you think about it anatomically, men "give" and women "receive."

This is why a lot of men need to feel like they can make a woman happy before they can form a bond. If he feels like she can't receive what he has to give, then he won't want to be with her.

Masculine energy is the world of unlimited potential—it's the iPhone, the ability to do infinite things at any time. Feminine energy manifests, it is taking that potential and actualizing it.

Masculine energy is focused, strong, goal-oriented, needs respect and freedom. Feminine energy is flowing, wants connection, nurtures relationships, and can actualize potential.

In my content, a man might connect to the way I describe women, or a woman may connect to the way I describe men, and that's normal!

The reason I use men and women is because most men have more of that masculine essence and most women, the feminine essence.

Qualities That Make Him The One

I don't mean to destroy your hopes and dreams, but a relationship is just having someone to do life with. And life is long and tedious and challenging (and also beautiful and meaningful and all that good stuff, but you really need to work to get to the good. The bad, unfortunately, comes easy). The best partner is one you can weather the storm with. In the beginning it was all so easy and so effortless, but the beginning is a gift and it's not reality.

It's easy to be the perfect partner when everything is going great and it's all so new and fresh and exciting. Just like it's easy to be the perfect parent when your children are behaving like little angels. But that's not reality. The reality is what it's like when things get hard, when someone isn't behaving exactly how you want them to, when you have to communicate about difficult issues, when your personalities clash, when you don't see eye to eye on important issues—then how do you cope? How do you relate to one another? How do you work as a team?

That's what to focus on because you can't date potential, you have to take someone as they are right now.

A lot of women write to me begging to understand why their relationships always fail...why guys treat them badly...why they always get hurt...why they can't get a guy to commit. The common thread in most of these cases is that these women are choosing men who clearly are not husband—or even relationship—material and hoping that by some chance the men will suddenly transform into the knights in shining armor they want. This type of situation doesn't exist anywhere aside from cheesy romantic comedies. If you choose to pursue a relationship with a guy who clearly isn't relationship material, then you're setting yourself up to fail before you even begin.

Trust me, I know all too well how enticing those damage cases can be. A damage case is my term for a guy who has a lot of potential buried under a pile of issues, and you make it your mission to clear the rubble to reveal the wonderful guy residing beneath.

Sure, he has emotional issues, he's jaded, he's struggling at work, he has no direction, he still acts like a frat boy even though his acting-like-a-drunk-idiot-and-getting-away-with-it days expired years ago, but there's a really great guy underneath all that and as soon as we deal with all this other stuff, *then* we'll have an amazing relationship. I'm sorry, but no.

The problem with these damage cases is that they often have a lot of the qualities we want, but not the ones we actually *need*. There is a big difference between wants and needs when it comes to relationships, but it's not always easy to make the distinction. You might want a guy who is tall and strapping and charismatic and a CEO of a major company, but a guy with those credentials might have a host of other qualities that aren't good for you and don't fulfill your fundamental emotional needs. My husband is the opposite of the "ideal man" I had envisioned for myself, but even though he doesn't have certain qualities I used to consider requirements, he is exactly what I need. That was clear to me and everyone around me very early into our relationship.

When I hit that stage in life where I realized I was done dating for the sake of dating and wanted to settle down and find "the one," I realized that the kinds of guys I liked to date weren't necessarily husband material, and I had to really examine my list of wants and needs and figure out the differences between the two. Doing so made all the difference. Suddenly the damage cases who were once *oh so appealing* did nothing for me.

Whether you're single, dating, or in a serious relationship, these are the most essential qualities you need to look for in a partner, the ones that tell you beyond a shadow of a doubt that he (or she) is the one and this is it.

> **He loves your good qualities and accepts and embraces the bad without making you feel guilty for having flaws.** You don't need to hide your true self from him and put on a front in order to be what you think he wants. You can share your true self and be vulnerable and feel safe doing

so, knowing that, if anything, it will make him feel even closer to you.

He is there for you when you need him, even if it's inconvenient for him. A partnership will sometimes require sacrifice and compromise. Life is unpredictable and unexpected. You can't predict what will happen and nothing can possibly go as planned 100% of the time. A guy who is husband material will be there for you when you need him. He will be in it with you; he will be your partner in whatever happens and will weather the storm with you, even though he might prefer to stay in the sunshine.

He considers you when making decisions, both big and small. A relationship is a partnership, not a dictatorship. Factoring you in shows that he respects you and that he wants to create a life with you, not simply envelope you in his world. Our worlds can be comfortable when we don't have to compromise, so it's not always easy taking someone else into account and factoring in their wants and needs and preferences, but that's what a relationship is.

He is growth oriented. No one is perfect; we all have flaws. And these flaws aren't black and white—usually a person's greatest strength is linked to his greatest weakness. In a relationship, his behavior affects you (and vice versa) and sometimes his less developed traits will have a negative impact on you. A growth-oriented guy will want to work to strengthen his character. A guy who isn't growth oriented will say it's your problem and that this is just the way he is and you need to deal with it.

For example, let's say you're dating a guy who can be insensitive at times. Maybe he doesn't give you emotional support when you've had a rough day and instead just gives you matter of fact advice in a direct way. His no-nonsense approach to solving problems might be useful to him in the workplace, but it might be hurtful to you sometimes when he doesn't empathize with what you're going through and instead just tells you what to do about it, or gets impatient by the fact that you're upset over something he doesn't consider to be that big of a deal.

You want a guy who will accept that his tone can come across as harsh and hurtful to you and who actually tries to work on it, not one who says it's your problem and you need to deal with it. He probably won't get it right every time, but if he's growth oriented he will at least try.

> **He has similar beliefs and values.** This one seems so obvious yet it's so often overlooked. Love does not in fact conquer all. If you are not fundamentally compatible, you will face major hurdles ahead. If he is going to be your life partner, you have to make sure you are both on the same page when it comes to issues that matter. And if you aren't on the same page, then make sure he respects where you stand (and vice versa) and that you're both willing to work together to reach a mutually fulfilling understanding about your differences.

Everyone's values are different. For some, their values will be rooted in religion. Other people value a strong work ethic, while some value a commitment to a healthy lifestyle. It may sound trivial, but I've seen very serious, long-term relationships end because one person couldn't deal with the other's lack of ambition or motivation.

> **He views you as his partner.** The relationship is something more than each of you individually...together, you and he are a team. And as that team, you are both individually stronger than you could be on your own. He sees you as his equal,

as a person of great value, someone he can grow with. Not someone who is there to feed his ego, give him validation, be his emotional crutch, or be there solely to satisfy his needs.

He respects everything about you—your thoughts, ambitions, opinions, the things you say, the company you keep, your job. He doesn't make you feel bad about your life circumstances and he appreciates the person you are and the choices you have made.

He wants to make you happy. One of a man's most fundamental needs in a relationship is to make his woman happy. It may not always feel like it or look like it, but it's true. In order to truly bond with a woman, a man needs to feel like he can make her happy. And when a man truly cares for a woman, he wants to do whatever it takes to make her happy. Love is a selfless thing. If you love people because they make you feel great about yourself, then it isn't real love. When a man shows he genuinely cares about you and your happiness, even if it sometimes comes at the expense of his own happiness, then you know his feelings are for real.

He communicates with you, even about tough issues and even if one of you is upset with the other. With the right guy, you won't be afraid of bringing up certain things for fear of rocking the boat. You know he respects you and will see what you have to say as valid and important. Every relationship will face its share of obstacles. There will be fights, miscommunications, arguments, and also times when one partner isn't feeling loved. The only way to emerge from the tough times better and stronger is to work through them together, and this starts with open communication.

He wants the same kind of commitment you want. A guy can have all the qualities on this list, but if he doesn't want to marry you (or commit in the way you want), or maybe

> doesn't want to get married in general, then he is not for you. When a guy is ready to get married and meets a girl he thinks he can spend his life with, he knows pretty early on. That's not to say he'll get engaged right away, but he knows this is it and she knows it too. Maybe he tells her or maybe it's so obvious he doesn't even need to. It might be the wrong time, maybe he wants to wait until he's more established in his career or more financially stable, but he will still convey his level of commitment; she won't be left hanging and guessing and wondering.

If he still feels like he has wild oats to sow and is drawn to the single, bachelor, party-boy lifestyle, he is not commitment minded and you are setting yourself up for disappointment. If what you want is a serious, lasting commitment, make sure he is on the same page before you become invested. When a guy is ready for a serious commitment, it's usually pretty obvious. And if it isn't, then bring it up and discuss it with him. If he's husband material, he'll understand. If he isn't...then at least now you know before it's too late! And yes, I understand that not every woman makes getting married a goal and I respect that. But I'm speaking to those who want a lasting commitment, be it marriage or a partnership without a legal piece of paper.

But The Most Important Quality Of All Is...

He wants to make it work. He's willing to put in any amount of effort. If there is a problem, he wants to find a way to solve it. He wants to work harder, to be better, to be his best self. The important thing to keep in mind is that people have different ideas about what it means to put effort into a relationship. He might believe that working hard and being good at his job is putting in effort because he wants to provide for you and give you nice things and a comfortable lifestyle. (I use this as an example because it's a classic point of contention between men and women: she will often view him working too much as him putting no effort into the relationship and being married to his work).

I remember the exact moment I knew my husband was the one. After about a month of everything being perfect (as they usually are in the beginning), we had our first conflict. It was nothing major; we just started experiencing areas where our personalities clashed and seeing how we process things differently. I tend to be more intellectual and straightforward in my thinking, while he's more emotional and dynamic in his thinking. I would get impatient with this, and my impatience was hurtful to him. The details don't really matter, what matters is that I remember the way he brought the issue up and how sincere he was about working through things and getting to a place of better understanding.

I have seen countless variations of this kind of scenario: a girl is dating a guy, things are going great (again, as they often do in the beginning), but then they hit that inevitable point of conflict. Maybe she acts needy or maybe he gets distant, but whatever happens suddenly things aren't as seamless as they were the week before. Then he decides he can't hang anymore and tells her he "doesn't have time for a relationship" or he can't give her what she needs. The girl racks her brain trying to figure out what she did wrong, what she could have done differently.

She thinks if she hadn't been so needy, if she had been a little more chilled out, if she hadn't done this and instead done that, then everything would have been fine. Really, the only way things would have turned out differently is if she had behaved perfectly according to his script, if she'd never disagreed or been unhappy with him, if she'd been perfectly in alignment with his thoughts and what he wanted in a partner. That sounds reasonable, right? (That's sarcasm in case it didn't come across!)

If a guy leaves when things get a little rocky, it means he is lacking in the most important quality you need in a partner, and that is commitment not only to you, but to making it work. It's easy to be in a relationship when everything is all sunshine and roses. The truth comes out after time goes on, when you let your guard down, when you can be more of yourselves. Even the best couples don't seamlessly fit together. There is always a certain degree of work involved in order to create that deep and meaningful connection, and it has to come from both people.

When a guy is ready to settle down and sees you as a good potential partner, he wants to make it work. He wants to overcome the differences, to get to a place of better understanding. My husband and I are so different. The way we think and feel is different, and the way we communicate is different. In the beginning of our relationship this definitely caused problems, but now, after really committing to working on it, we have hit this amazing place of understanding and are so much more in sync. The differences still exist, but we were able to meet in the middle. Even when things got difficult, I wasn't any less sure he was the guy for me because of how deeply committed he was to making it work.

A big mistake I see women making is blaming themselves when a relationship falls apart. They torture themselves with could haves and should haves. I should have been less needy, I should have been more agreeable, I could have been more supportive, etc. Yeah, you could have done all that, but it wouldn't have mattered if he wasn't committed to making it work.

There will always be differences, there will always be problems, you will not always behave exactly how he wants a partner to behave (same for him).

A relationship isn't about finding the perfect match, it's about finding someone you can form a meaningful, lasting partnership with. Notice the word *form*. It's an active process; it doesn't just exist. It's about working together, being a team, and overcoming the challenges.

Some people have deal-breakers and that's that. Maybe it's religion or where to live or lifestyle preferences. But all the other stuff—personality quirks, your nature, your ways of interacting in social settings, your fundamental traits...either he's in it or he's not. And if he's not, then there is nothing you can do.

Red Flags You Should Never Ignore

Every relationship is different and comes with a unique set of circumstances. However, there are some universal standards that indicate a person isn't the right one for you, a few red flags that should never be ignored but usually are.

You Don't Trust Them

Without trust, there is no relationship. Period. In a good, strong, healthy relationship, you feel at ease. You feel safe. You feel secure. You do not feel constantly panicked and on edge, always anticipating the proverbial other shoe to drop.

If you don't believe the things he tells you or are always questioning his motives and his whereabouts, there is something majorly amiss. You can't spend your life constantly on the lookout; that's just exhausting.

Sometimes a lack of trust develops because of something substantial. Maybe he cheated, maybe you caught him in a few too many lies. And sometimes it's something that lingers in the pit of your gut. Even though you can't quantify the reason, you just don't feel like you can trust this person. Either way, it's a big red flag and a major sign that your relationship isn't going to last.

If he cheated on you or lied to you, then you'll have to be honest with yourself when you decide if you can truly move past it and if you really, genuinely believe that he'll never do the same thing again. If you can't get to that place, then there isn't much point in sticking it out. You're just setting yourself up for a life in which you always feel paranoid and insecure. Relationships are supposed to bring out your best, not your worst.

If you can't quite pinpoint the reason for your trust issues, you should listen to your gut. Our gut instincts can be incredibly powerful. Just make sure you aren't projecting your own insecurities onto him and aren't making him pay for the sins of a cheating/lying ex.

There Is No Depth Of Connection

Sexual chemistry is great and is definitely important, but that alone can't sustain a relationship. An amazing sex life is only one piece of the puzzle, yet for a lot of couples it's the only leg the relationship has to stand on. I know so, *so* many women who got so engulfed by the intoxicating chemistry they experienced with their partner that they overlooked every sign that clearly showed he wasn't the one...and wasn't even that great of a person.

For a relationship to last, you need to have depth of connection. You need to know your partner intimately, and this goes way beyond his bedroom skills. You need to know who he is, what he wants out of life, and what his hopes, dreams, and fears are. You need to connect to each other in an honest, unguarded way.

Each person is composed of many layers. In our lives, some people see the surface layer, a select few see what lies beneath the exterior, and very few see straight to the core. Your life partner should be in the last group.

Knowing the basics about someone isn't knowing who they are. If you know the same things about your guy as most of the other people in his life, then you don't have much depth of connection.

Fortunately, this issue is one that can be fixed. Try to make an effort to connect to him in a real way. If he resists, or you still don't feel like you're connecting in a significant way, then it means he's probably not that invested in you or the relationship. Or maybe you're just not the right fit for one another.

Attraction and sexual chemistry are never enough to sustain a relationship. If that's all you have that's fine, but you might want to move on if you're serious about finding the one.

Lack Of Respect

Respect is the most overlooked element when it comes to making a relationship work, but it's one of the most essential. If you're going to have a long-lasting, healthy relationship, you must respect your partner and he must respect you.

Respect is huge for guys. In fact, I'd say it's the number one thing men want out of their relationship. Just as most women need to feel loved and adored, men need to feel respected and admired. A man needs to feel like *the man*; he needs to feel respected. If you don't respect him or the way he lives his life, he will resent you and will not want to be with you long term.

At the same time, you need to be with a partner who respects you. This means he respects you as a person: your beliefs, your aspirations, and especially your boundaries.

Famed researcher John Gottman identified four horsemen that predict divorce: criticism, contempt, defensiveness, and stonewalling.

Of the four, he identified contempt as the most destructive. Expressions of contempt such as eye-rolling, sneering, mimicking, and name calling have proven to be the biggest predictors of divorce in his over four decades of research.

Contempt is the opposite of respect. Contempt says, "I'm better than you. And you are lesser than me."

He Brings Out Your Worst

As I mentioned earlier, relationships are supposed to bring out your best. The sad fact is, a lot of women end up shackled to a person who brings out their worst.

Sometimes you might not even recognize the person that your relationship has turned you into. That was definitely the case for me many years back before I knew any better. I made the same mistake countless women make. I got so caught up in my feelings for the guy that I overlooked the fact that I didn't really like myself all that much when I was around him.

I was unrecognizable from my previous confident, happy, positive self. Instead I felt insecure, panicked, anxious, and perpetually on edge, but I couldn't let go because of my strong feelings for him. Those feelings locked me in a tight grip, and it was only when the relationship inevitably imploded that I was able to see just how toxic the situation truly was.

It wasn't that he was a bad guy; he was just bad for me. It's a fact that would have saved me years of heartache had I realized it sooner. While getting myself out of that relationship felt impossible, the end was always inevitable because we brought out the worst in each other.

The point is, a relationship should lift you higher, not drag you down. It should help you reach your potential and become a better version of yourself. Of course relationships can't be perfect all the time. They take patience and work. But this work leads to a positive place, a place of growth and understanding and more love and connection. Bad relationships are ones where the work involved is expending energy on fighting and arguing and trying to win. A relationship won't always feel perfect and pleasant, but overall it will help you grow into a better person, as long as you're with a good guy who is committed to making it work and loves and appreciates you for who you are.

He Doesn't Take Responsibility

One of the biggest relationship red flags is when someone won't take responsibility for anything and instead blames you, maybe using a justification along the lines of, "Well I wouldn't yell at you if you weren't being so annoying." Rather than admitting when he's wrong, he comes up with excuses and justifications for his behaviors and reasons to blame you.

One of the biggest indicators of psychopaths or sociopaths is not being able to take responsibility; it's a fundamental lack of empathy that prevents them from ever being able to see the other person's perspective. However, it doesn't always start out this way. In the beginning he's enraptured by you and everything you do is right. Then suddenly he's unhappy and he blames you for everything that's wrong. If you erroneously reason that you're the problem, he may feed this mentality. You don't inspire him enough, you don't give him what he needs, you aren't supportive enough, you're always negative. It's always you, never him.

I'm not saying every guy who can't take responsibility is a psycho; he could just be immature. But it is something to keep in mind because narcissists are out there and this is one of their key features.

He's Selfish

I have a friend who was seeing a guy she really liked, and she continued to date him even though he was clearly a bit immature and selfish and not ready to settle down (we joked that he had her *sexmotized* and that's why she wasn't able to break free of his spell). There were signs of trouble all over the place, but most were little things and that's why they were easy to sweep under the rug.

For example, one night she suggested they go to a vegetarian Indian restaurant she loved, and he got all pissy and said there wasn't a point in going out for Indian food if he couldn't eat meat. Never mind the fact that he always chose the restaurants, that they always did what he wanted, that they always slept at his apartment because that's what he wanted, or the fact that he had told her to pick a place for dinner. It was the one time she got to decide something, and she was overruled because it wasn't what he wanted.

This may seem like a silly example, but it demonstrates the essence of selfishness, one that will continue to pop up when dealing with a selfish person. And in that relationship, it did, over and over until finally she couldn't take it anymore and ended it. (This launched the make-up and break-up cycle for a while, because that's what happens when you linger in a relationship with the wrong guy, but eventually they cut it off for good.)

Selfish people also tend to engage in selfish love. That is, they love you when you make them feel good; when you're behaving how they want you to, they're the best partners ever. When you go off script, then they withdraw and won't do anything for you in a sort of tit-for-tat retaliation.

That's not how a relationship works. A relationship isn't there to serve one person. It's a partnership and it's about working together, not one person working for the other.

Let Your Gut Be Your Guide

I mentioned the importance of listening to your gut earlier and want to get into it a little deeper because it's an essential skill, one that can keep you out of sticky situations.

I have been a relationship writer and coach for a long time now and the majority of the time, when a woman comes to me with a relationship question...she already knows the answer, she just wishes she didn't because it doesn't align with how she wants things to be. People usually come to me hoping they're wrong, but they already know what I'm going to say before I say it. Because deep down, you already know the truth.

The list I provided of qualities to look for and red flags to watch out for can help you see things more clearly, maybe making it harder to hide from what's right in front of you, but oftentimes you already know. You know when a guy isn't worthy of you—when you're wasting your time, when you're not being treated the way you would like to be treated or the way you know you deserve to be treated—but you push this knowledge down because you just don't want to deal with it. You don't want to deal with a breakup, with putting yourself back on the market, with dating more guys, navigating the waters, trying to find a guy who cares about you. You don't want to because it's exhausting! It seems somehow easier to stick with what's broken and try to just make it work.

In a good, strong, healthy relationship, you feel loved and secure. You don't question whether your man is using you and if the things he says are genuine. You just feel at ease. Feeling constantly on edge, waiting anxiously for the other shoe to drop, is usually a sign that something is amiss and your instincts are trying to open your eyes to a reality you don't want to see.

Your gut is a powerful tool in relationships. It's something we all possess and it can be fine-tuned to work optimally. The way to get in touch with it is to listen to what it's telling you. Listen to that small, quiet voice that gently tells you: "You deserve more than this, you don't need this guy."

The voice of your ego is loud and overpowering. It tells you "Of course he's the guy for you! So what if he disappears for days at a time, he told you that you were the most amazing woman he's ever met, so I mean, DUH! He loves you."

Your ego shouts over the noise and convinces you that the outcome you want is reality because it has a lot at stake should this not be the case.

Most people allow their egos to get so entangled in their relationships that when the relationship collapses, their ego comes crashing down with it and then absolute misery ensues.

Our unconscious mind has a whole arsenal of information that our conscious mind doesn't have easy access to. It has stored up pretty much everything that's ever happened to us and makes decisions accordingly.

Have you ever met someone and liked him right away even though you barely knew him? Or maybe you meet someone who seems perfectly nice, but you just can't stand her? This is the unconscious at work. The people we are drawn to oftentimes remind us of people we've had positive encounters with in the past. So too with the people we don't like right off the bat.

You can pick up on things subconsciously without even realizing it, and it will cause you to have a feeling that you can't quite pinpoint or explain.

The point is, most of the time you already know the answer. The problem is that you wish it were a different answer so instead of accepting it you whittle away what you know with rationalizations.

Here are a few tips to help you get better acquainted with your gut:

Ask yourself a question and listen for the immediate answer. For example, if you're debating whether or not to dump your boyfriend, ask yourself: "Should I break up with him?," and listen to what first pops into your head. The real answer will most often come first, and then the excuses and justifications will pile on top.

Make the decision and then listen to your body. If it's a bad decision you'll feel an aversion to it, usually in the pit of your stomach.

Check with a friend. It can help to get an outsider's perspective because sometimes we can mistake wishful thinking for our gut instincts. Talk to a friend you trust for a dose of objectivity.

Practice mindfulness. Most people live their lives bouncing from one thing to the next—work, errands, gym, happy hour. There isn't that much time to listen to our own thoughts. Try to stay mindful and conscious throughout the day and check in with yourself to see what you're thinking and feeling. It also helps to set aside some reflection time. You can use this time to meditate, do yoga, journal, take a walk around the park—anything that will give you the space to check in with yourself.

Remember this: Choice is everything. It will largely determine if a relationship succeeds and lasts or fails and leaves you broken-hearted. The good news is that you have the power to choose the man you let into your life. Choose wisely!

CHAPTER 2

What Is Love, Anyway?

"We always believe our first love is our last, and our last love our first." —*George John Whyte-Melville*

When I was younger, I couldn't *wait* to fall in love. I vividly remember getting frozen yogurt with a group of girl friends when we were in middle school and one of my friends saying, "Guys, how excited are you to fall in love?" The rest of us couldn't help but giggle at the silliness of her statement...but we all felt an undeniable rush of excitement over the prospect and nodded in agreement.

One of my exes, whom I loved with all my heart, with every fiber of my being...let me tell you, it was nothing like the movies. While he loved me very much, there were too many other variables that stood in our way, and the relationship was always strained and on the brink of implosion. We had maybe a month of being drunk on love...and then almost a year of pain and problems. I didn't understand; *this isn't how it's supposed to be.* The challenges and differences aren't supposed to matter...it's supposed to all just work itself out and then you make promises of forever and you keep them, and of course a happily ever after is the expected and rightful reward for making it through the storm.

The last thing in the world I ever anticipated was for my "one true love" to so abruptly fall out of love with me...and fall in love with someone else. It left me broken, jaded, and utterly confused. Was it not really love? It sure felt like it, but true love is supposed to last forever, isn't it?

The reason so many of us have a hard time recognizing real love and making a relationship last is because most of us don't get any formal education in these areas; instead, our beliefs and ideas about love come from the mainstream media...not exactly the most reliable source! And even if we ignore all that, many of us learn faulty and unreliable ideas about love from our parents and families. We might eventually learn to recognize certain things as unhealthy or even dysfunctional, but that doesn't mean we have a clue what healthy and functional looks like!

So let's break it down and uncover the truth about love and relationships, the good and the bad.

Top Five Biggest Misconceptions About Love

I'd say just about every person on the planet is seeking, or trying to maintain, lasting love. The problem is most of us have long-standing, firmly ingrained, highly unrealistic ideas of what love is *supposed* to be, and feel frustrated when reality falls short.

No one would deny that love is a beautiful, transformative experience, but at the same time, it's important to have a realistic understanding of what it actually is.

Here are some of the biggest myths about what love is:

Misconception #1
It's Supposed To Be Difficult

The predominant depiction of love in movies and on TV is that it's supposed to be a challenge, something you fight for at all costs and don't ever give up on. While this certainly makes for good entertainment, it's not a realistic portrayal of love.

Relationships do take work, but falling in love (in a healthy way) is a relatively effortless process. It's not filled with hours of analyzing what he meant when he said XYZ, or feeling a sense of impending doom at all times, or making grand sacrifices and compromising who you are for the sake of the one you love. Who can forget the final scene in "Grease" when Sandy ditches the poodle skirt and sweater set for second-skin black leggings, an edgy bomber jacket, and a cigarette between her lips while Danny literally falls at her feet, overcome by pure lust and a need to have her right there in the carnival fun-house.

This is *not* what love looks like! When someone truly loves you, you will not have to mold yourself in order to fit with him; the pieces will naturally click.

The drama so often associated with love usually only applies to unhealthy relationships: ones that result from infatuation, obsession, or unrealistic expectations, not a genuine connection. A healthy, loving relationship is one where two people can be their authentic selves and look at what they can give to the relationship, rather than what they can get from it. Both people complement each other and are able to give what the other needs and happily receive what their partner has to give. You should never have to fight for someone's love, or plot ways to make someone love you. When it's real and genuine, it will flow easily and effortlessly.

Misconception #2
Love Conquers All

From music to movies to literature, everywhere you turn in mainstream media you hear love is all you need, love conquers all, love lifts us up where we belong...I could go on and on. Love is for sure a beautiful thing. Love is also necessary in order for a relationship to last, but it's not enough. Sometimes two people just don't fit. It's unfortunate, but it's a fact.

The reason most people are so jaded is they stay in relationships that aren't working for way too long. They try to be what the other person needs, they try to make it work by any means necessary, they try with all their might and they wind up broken and defeated. You simply cannot shove a square peg into a round hole. It doesn't matter how many ways you try, you will never be able to make it fit.

There's this idea that if you love someone enough, it will just work out. But sometimes it doesn't. It doesn't mean your love wasn't real, it just means that there were other factors at play and as a result, it just couldn't work long term.

While love is very powerful and capable of conquering some things, it isn't always strong enough to conquer other things, like different backgrounds, values, goals, and visions for the future, for example. Most of all, love simply cannot conquer incompatibility.

Misconception #3
Only True Love Lasts

An important truth to realize is that not all love is meant to last; sometimes it's just part of the journey. Loving someone does not mean they are the right person for you. It doesn't guarantee you a happily ever after. More often than love leading to marriage, love leads to heartbreak...but the heartbreak can lead to growth, and that growth can lead to another love, one that can lead to a lasting marriage.

I have loved several wrong people in my life. While some of those experiences left me with a lot of shattered pieces to put back together, time has shown that none of those guys were right for me. It doesn't mean the love we shared was flawed or not enough, it just means we weren't compatible.

The sad fact is that many relationships end with bitterness and hate. One or both people leave the relationship thinking they were owed something, and they blame the other for not following through on this unwritten promise. If we could all just realize that love does not guarantee a happy ending, we would be able to move forward much more easily and start a new relationship with an open heart, rather than one shrouded in pain and disappointment.

Misconception #4
You "Just Know" When It's Right

One of the biggest misconceptions about love is that you "just know" when you find the "right one." This mentality frees you of all responsibility in your love life; you don't need to work on yourself or prepare for love, just go about your business and someday the right one will drop into your life and you'll just know.

In order to fall in love with the right person, you need to be in the right place emotionally. If you don't find love from within, you will never be able to let it in from the outside. But no one likes to talk about this because it takes work, and the idea of some perfect person just entering your life and being the other half of you, the yin to your yang, is just so much easier and far more romantic.

In order to correctly identify the right one for you, you need to know who you are. You need to know your values, your boundaries, your fundamental needs, your wants, what you can compromise on, and what your absolute deal-breakers are. When you are in this place and the right person comes along, the one who understands you and sees you and connects with you and can give you what you need in a relationship, it will feel right and you will just *know*...but only because you've prepared yourself for love and are in the right place emotionally.

It's also worth noting that love is something that can grow over time; there aren't always instant fireworks that erupt as soon as your eyes meet. Often women reject perfectly good guys after a few dates because they "just didn't feel it." I'm not saying you should settle, but I am saying you should adjust your idea of what love should feel like. I know plenty of happily married women who almost didn't give their now husbands a second date. I'm not saying love at first sight can't, or doesn't, ever happen—it does, I've seen it—but it doesn't guarantee you a happier, more fulfilling relationship. It's just another means to get to the same destination, one that can be just as easily achieved slowly. (Side note: what we call "love at first sight" is really intense lust and desire coupled with the recognition that there is the potential to create something meaningful with this other person. You can't possibly know someone well enough on the first date to actually love him, but you can recognize the potential to create love with him.)

Often we reject the guys who would be good to us (and for us) because we are not yet in a place where we can receive true love. Instead we feel drawn to the guys who are unavailable, and we get caught up in trying to prove our worth and show him we're good enough. This toxic dating style happens when you don't feel worthy of love on some level...and going after these kinds of guys validates that notion.

The funny thing about the human mind, whether you realize it or not, is that it's always looking to validate beliefs, no matter how damaging those beliefs are. If you believe no one likes you, your mind will ignore all the evidence that you are likable and will hone in on only those specific incidents when someone rejected you.

A big part of preparing yourself for love is letting go of resentments from the past, whether they stem from problems with ex-boyfriends, your parents, or your friends. Make an effort to let go of any lingering resentment you feel, because the truth is that holding onto this negativity is hurting you more than anyone else. When you hold onto faulty beliefs such as, "All men are commitment-phobes" or "The guys I like always dump me," you sow the seeds for self-fulfilling prophecies.

For example, when you carry the idea around that all men are afraid of commitment, you will instinctively put up walls and won't trust the guys you date. As a result, you will never be able to get to that level of openness and trust necessary to create the kind of connection that leads to love. This doesn't only apply to relationships, this applies to every area of your life. Thoughts breed reality.

Misconception #5
Love Is All You Need

When we think of what it takes to have a lasting, happy relationship, we of course say love is the most essential ingredient. Next usually comes good communication, shared goals, and the like. But no one ever talks about the importance of lust.

Love and lust are often painted as opposites, with the former being pure, transcendent, and full of light while the latter is depraved and full of darkness. They say love is giving, lust is taking; love is selfless, lust is selfish. While in its pure, isolated state lust can be a negative thing, so can love (at least, in romantic relationships). When your relationship is pure love, you have a level of comfort and familiarity.

Married people and couples who live together know what this is like. You love your partner very much, and can be completely comfortable around him...but sometimes things become a little *too* comfortable and the passion you once felt is nowhere to be found. This isn't the result of lack of love; it's lack of lust.

When you are in an established relationship, you shouldn't just sit back, sink into complacency, and assume he'll just love you unconditionally. This is true to an extent, but if you want to keep the flames burning, you have to work on maintaining that level of lust. One of the most common reasons for breakups is the old, "I love you, I'm just not in love with you." Usually what this means is "I no longer feel that lustful passion for you. I love you...but in the same way I love my family and close friends."

In a romantic relationship, love will give you stability, partnership, and acceptance, but lust will give you passion, fire, and sexual satisfaction.

While love is about accessibility and constant companionship, lust is a bit more forbidden; it's about wanting rather than having.

There are many ways to keep the lust alive in your relationship; you'll probably discover them all by just thinking about how things were in the beginning of your relationship, back when you were overcome by a magnetic force of physical attraction. Try to maintain some mystery when you can and get back in touch with your more sexual side. Instead of going to bed in a ratty tee shirt and shorts, invest in some sexy sleepwear. When you know he's coming home from work, change out of your sweats and wear something alluring. It's not easy, I know that. I have three young children and exist in a permanent state of haggard, and sometimes that's just what it is, but when I make the effort to get back in touch with that sensual side of myself that came so naturally before children, there is a measurable difference in my relationship.

There are countless ways to bring the spark back into a relationship, so just play around and see what does the trick for you!

The Ugly Truth

About Relationships

When you're single, it's easy to fall into the trap of thinking that everything will be perfect when you find the right guy. I'll admit that I was once guilty of this line of thinking. It can seem like a relationship is that one missing piece and once you have it, you will finally have it all. Then maybe you meet a guy, you click, you start dating, and all seems to be running smoothly until certain unpleasant realities of being in a relationship start to creep in, either slowly and by degrees or quickly and all at once.

Relationships take work; there is no way around that. You can be totally perfect for one another, you can love each other like crazy, you can be wildly attracted to one another, you can even be soulmates, and you will still have to work at it. When you're in a relationship, it isn't just about you anymore. Your choices, your actions, your behavior, your tone of voice, your mood and so forth, they all affect someone else (and vice versa). A relationship is a partnership, and having a partner is amazing in many ways, but it also means there is someone else in the picture who matters. And like you, he also comes with a fair amount of baggage, issues, unresolved pain from the past, etc.

When a relationship starts to get real, it can be confusing and overwhelming. You may wonder if you've made a mistake, if maybe this isn't the right relationship. You may feel wronged because *this isn't how it's supposed to be.* All relationships will hit points where you struggle, and actually, the struggles are a good thing. When handled right, they can make you even stronger as a couple. But when dealt with improperly, they can cause irreparable harm (to both you and the relationship).

Here are five not-so-fun facts you must face about being in a relationship:

1. Fights Are Inevitable

Fighting with the person you love is profoundly painful, but it's inevitable and sometimes it's necessary. It can also be a brutal reality check. In the beginning of a relationship I think almost every woman has moments when she thinks, "Wow, this guy is amazing. He gets me and I love him so much, what could we ever fight about? Maybe other couples fight, but that will never be us." And you might really believe it; you might wonder what you could ever possibly fight about. But in time, this idealism gets shattered and you are forced to face some of the unpleasant realities of being in a relationship.

It's important to realize that even the most compatible couple will sometimes disagree, and these disagreements can escalate into arguments and full-fledged fights.

Your goal shouldn't be to never fight; it should be to fight better. Learn to fight in a way that brings about resolution rather than dissolution. A fight doesn't have to include yelling and screaming and slamming doors and hurling insults and trying to make the other person feel as bad as they made you feel. It is very difficult to come to a place of resolution when emotions are running hot, so one of the best tips to fight better is to stop discussing an issue until both of you have had the chance to reset your systems back to neutral. Whenever a conflict emerges, it is also helpful to remind yourself, and each other, that you are both on the same team and that you should try to work with each other instead of against each other.

2. The First To Say Sorry Is Actually The Stronger One

This point picks up where I left off in the first reality check. You and he are on the same team and you're fighting for the same cause, the cause being to have a healthy, happy, loving, mutually fulfilling relationship. When you make yourself the victim and him the victimizer, you aren't on the same team, you are opponents locked in a battle to prove that you're right and the other person is wrong. This puts the other person on the defensive, and he may launch a counterattack that only confirms for you that he is completely at fault, and from there it spirals into an ugly place.

Maybe you're right and maybe you do want to "win" the argument, but if you end up tearing each other down to do it, then you both lose.

Sometimes, you just need to suck it up and say, "I'm sorry we fought" or "I'm sorry you were hurt." Maybe you think he's being irrational and you don't think he's justified in feeling the way he's feeling, and maybe you're right, but it doesn't matter who's right. What should matter more is the fact that the person you love is hurt, and you can be sorry for hurting him even if you don't fully understand where he's coming from.

If he did something that hurt you, try to express that to him in a way that doesn't make him feel attacked. This is totally achievable when you're coming from a place of genuinely wanting the relationship to work and wanting to connect and share your perspective with him so the relationship will improve, and not from a place of trying to be the victor.

Sometimes he'll do something that hurts you, and you'll think he was completely in the wrong, while he'll think you're in the wrong for being upset. I'm not referring to clear-cut wrongdoing like cheating, but something along the lines of you had a bad day and wanted to spend time alone with him, but he already had plans and didn't want to cancel. You may feel he should prioritize you and cancel those plans, but he doesn't like to be the kind of person who flakes when he says he's going to do something. It doesn't matter who is right and who is wrong, and in reality, both people are usually a little of both. Trying to prove your case will get you nowhere.

3. Resentment Will Crop Up

Resentment is by far the number-one relationship killer. Resentment is what causes couples to fall out of love, to stop desiring one another, to fight constantly over everything. As a relationship progresses, the number of minor hurts will accumulate. That time he blew off date night to hang out with his friends...that time he forgot about important plans...that time he said something hurtful...that time you had a fight and he didn't say sorry...

Whether your relationship survives and blossoms or deteriorates and implodes comes down to what you do with all those hurts. In a relationship, you will get hurt sometimes, even if you're with the sweetest, most loving man in the world. He usually won't mean it; he may not even realize something he said or did was insensitive or hurtful. Maybe you say something about it, maybe you don't. Sometimes you can get over something on your own (especially if it was something innocent that you overreacted about because of your own insecurity), sometimes an apology is necessary, and sometimes a serious "relationship talk" is needed.

If you don't deal with your hurts properly, they will build up within you and morph into resentment. Once the seeds of resentment have been planted, every minor thing he does will feed them and cause them to grow, even the things that you know objectively aren't that big of a deal. The more resentment grows, the more it will poison the relationship.

You may silently punish him in retribution, which will cause him to feel resentful towards you, which will cause you to feel more resentment towards him. This is how the vicious ugly cycle begins, and things get very complicated very fast.

Sometimes you will be extremely hurt. Even if he apologized in the most sincere, loving way, you won't be able to fully forgive and definitely won't forget. You may appreciate the apology, you may accept it, but in your mind you may be thinking, "I still can't believe he would say something like that! How could he?!" So it's still there, it's still with you, and the next time an issue comes up, you'll use it as ammo against him.

When you've been hurt you are faced with a choice: hold onto it and stay hurt, or just let it go. Maybe a part of you believes he doesn't deserve your full forgiveness, maybe you don't think he deserves to get your full love and affection, maybe you're still hurt. That will happen sometimes, but you need to realize that holding onto these bad feelings doesn't help you or your relationship. They keep you stuck in a negative place instead of moving forward, and if you can't move past a conflict then you will forever be in it, and who wants that? Even if he doesn't "deserve" to be fully forgiven, make the choice to just let it go and realize that working on improving things in the future is much better that staying angry over what happened in the past.

Again, I should mention that certain things are unforgivable and I'm not talking about those things. I'm not talking about cheating or violence or something purposefully done out of malice. I'm talking about the small little hurts that rack up over time. They are the shades of gray, not the black and whites.

4. It Will Be Challenging At Times

Relationships take work, there is no way around it. A relationship is like a plant; it needs proper, consistent care or it will wither and die. And sometimes it will be really tough. There will be times when you can't seem to communicate, times when you feel disconnected and angry, times when you start to question everything. These times will become few and far between if you put in the right amount of work. This includes releasing resentments from arguments past, letting go of the need to always be right, and realizing that certain issues won't ever be resolved and you're beating a dead horse trying.

A relationship is a partnership; it's two people coming together to share a life. However, these two people once had very separate, individual lives. They have different likes and preferences. They have different ways of dealing with things. They have different needs, different perspectives, and different values. Sometimes two people will be very compatible and will have the same views on where to live, what to spend money on, etc. For other couples, it will take a little more effort to bridge the gap.

The challenging aspects of a relationship subside when both people learn the importance of compromising and learning to see the world through their partner's eyes. You won't ever be able to inhabit his perspective, but you can try to understand it and validate it, and this is what builds a cohesive unit, when both people face challenges together instead of from opposite sides of the ring.

5. Sometimes, You're The Problem

This just might be the hardest reality check of all. Nobody wants to be the problem. It's much easier to blame someone else than admit you have issues to deal with, because dealing with issues is unpleasant and requires hard work. It's easy to blame someone for making you feel a certain way, but the reality is that oftentimes, you already felt that way. If you blame your boyfriend for "making you" feel insecure, you probably already feel insecure, and because of that you interpreted something innocent he said or did as critical.

We all have a certain degree of baggage, and most of our issues will rise to the surface in a relationship because love touches the deepest, most rarely accessed parts of our beings. Sometimes this can be beautiful and euphoric and other times it can be very painful because it brings up feelings and issues that we would rather not deal with. And so sometimes rather than dealing with them, we blame our guy for making us feel that way.

I'm not saying he's never at fault; sometimes he might be insensitive or hurtful (hopefully unintentionally). The point I'm making is that it's important to try to identify where the issue is really coming from. Is it him or is it you? Is he really not making you feel secure in the relationship or do you have some deep-seated intimacy issues to deal with? Does he really not make you feel loved, or do you not love yourself, and as a result are unable to let any love in from the outside?

The first step in having a healthy relationship is always to work on being your best self. This means being honest with yourself, looking at who you are and who you want to be, and dealing with anything that is getting in the way of that. Your partner can help you get there, but he can't do it for you. Only you control your emotional well-being.

Relationships can be tough at times, but when you're with the right partner, the work is so worth it. A healthy, loving relationship can enhance your life enormously and help you become your absolute best self. The path there isn't always smooth, but it is unquestionably worth it.

When Love Goes Wrong: Toxic Relationships

Something I and many other women know a lot about is toxic relationships. A toxic substance is something that causes damage to you, drains you, depletes you. A toxic relationship operates exactly like this and can irrevocably damage your sense of self.

There are toxic relationships and then there are *toxic relationships*, and one of my previous relationships fell into the latter.

It was only when the relationship inevitably imploded that I was able to see just how toxic the situation had been and how badly it had damaged my sense of self. Part of the reason I didn't see it sooner is that I didn't know what to look for. I let my strong feelings for him blind me to everything else. My friends tried to warn me that this was a bad situation, and so I stopped talking to them. My gut told me this was a bad situation, and so I stopped listening to it. I did what many do. I chose not to see things as they were and instead focused on how I wanted things to be. I minimized all that was bad and clung tightly to whatever scraps of good I could find, and that was all I needed to keep going.

The pain stayed with me long after the relationship was over, and those wounds took a very long time to heal. The trouble with toxic relationships is that they aren't always so easy to identify when you're in them, and sometimes it can even feel like you're being a drama queen to call it "toxic."

Maybe you think you're experiencing the typical ups and downs that relationships bring, or maybe you blame some external source and think that as soon as it gets resolved, everything will be fine.

It's not just a problem in romantic relationships. You can have toxic friends, family members, co-workers, bosses.

Being able to see a situation for what it is and accept that it isn't going to change can be empowering. It gives you the ability to look at things through an objective lens and make a decision that is in your best interest. Sometimes that means ending a romantic relationship or friendship. Maybe you find the strength to leave your job and find a new one. Maybe you realize you need to put up stronger boundaries around certain family members. Knowing what's going on is the first step to dealing with it.

To help you get there, I have identified the five biggest signs that you're in an emotionally toxic relationship.

1. You Never Feel Good Enough

You feel like nothing you ever do is quite right and are constantly trying to prove your worth. You become addicted to his validation. Whenever you do something and it generates any sort of approval from him, you feel relieved and it gives you just enough rope to hang onto. You try even harder to get more of that feeling, then feel like a failure when it doesn't come. No matter how hard you try, you never feel like you're enough or like you're doing things right. You live in a constant state of unease, of second-guessing yourself, of trying to be better and good enough.

2. You Can't Be Yourself

One sign that you're in a healthy, loving relationship is the feeling that you can just *be*. A big sign that you are in an unhealthy, toxic relationship is the opposite, the feeling that you can't be yourself. Instead, you have to walk on eggshells and monitor everything you say and do. You feel like you need to think twice before you speak and that certain topics are off limits, that you have to act a certain way. You are afraid to bring things up to him because you don't know how he'll react, and saying nothing is better than saying something and having him get angry. So you suffer in silence and hope that things will change, that somehow this relationship will magically transform into a healthy, happy one.

You may not even recognize the person this relationship is turning you into. You wonder why you're not the same cool, fun, confident woman anymore, and maybe your friends and family feel the same. But you love him and you've invested this much into the relationship and you reason that as soon as you get through this rough patch, you'll go back to being that girl again...

3. He Puts You Down

This is one of the biggest signs of a toxic relationship, and it seems like it would be pretty black and white, but often you don't even realize all the ways he's putting you down because it can be done in sneaky ways that aren't flat-out criticisms. And if you're in far enough, you already aren't feeling like yourself and aren't feeling good enough about yourself, so you may even agree with the negative things he says to you and about you.

Relationships are a chance for enormous personal growth. Sometimes our less-than-stellar qualities are brought to the surface and they need to be dealt with. However, there is a huge difference between a partner who can point out your flaws in a loving way, a way that encourages you to grow, and a partner who does it from a place of contempt. In a healthy relationship, he will accept you for who you are. He will love the good and accept the bad because we're all human and we're all flawed, and bad qualities just come with the territory.

In a healthy relationship, you will want to improve because you genuinely want to be your best self—for your sake, for his sake, and for the sake of the relationship. You will feel loved and accepted for who you are, and both you and he will understand that change takes time, so you won't feel bad about succumbing to some of your negative qualities from time to time.

In a toxic relationship, you won't feel accepted, your partner will have little tolerance for your negative qualities, and he may shame you and belittle you for them.

I remember early in a former toxic relationship, my ex told me that the reason he chose me was because he knew he could never "breed with" (yes, that's a direct quote) someone like me because I wasn't really wife and mother material (mind you, I was a 20-year-old college kid), so it made him feel safe knowing that this relationship wouldn't be forever. Your jaw may have dropped reading that, and maybe you're thinking "Well of course she left him after that," but I didn't! I remember feeling shame and embarrassment that I liked to go out and party (again, I was 20!), and I made it my mission to prove to him what a nurturer I could be. I was always on a mission to prove something to him, I could never just *be*.

In a toxic relationship, put-downs run rampant. Some are overt and others are masked and both will make you feel bad, but you may not fully recognize the long-term internal damage they are causing.

4. You Fight Dirty

Couples fight, even the happiest ones, it just comes with the territory. Fights can occur over all sorts of things, both big and small. Happy couples aren't ones who never fight, they are ones who use fights and disagreements as a means to *resolve the issue.* If something can't be resolved, they learn how to communicate better and reach a place of deeper understanding.

Toxic couples usually fight to win. They use fights as an opportunity to tear the other person down, to hit below the belt, to get out all the anger and resentment they feel. Dirty fights are a sign that the resentment level in the relationship has hit its limit. These fights are full of hostility and contempt, and each person is overcome by the desire to "win" and prove their case rather than work together to lovingly resolve the issue.

5. He Won't Work On It

He doesn't take responsibility and instead blames you and makes it all your fault. (He says things like, "Well I wouldn't get so angry if you weren't always on my case!") In a toxic relationship, you feel like the problem. He doesn't value your feelings or your needs. If you're upset, it's because you're too "sensitive" or "emotional" or "irrational." He may say he's sorry, but he doesn't really own up to anything and thinks if you have a problem with the relationship then it's just that, *your* problem. He doesn't want to talk about it or work on it or try to change.

He may also gaslight you so you don't know which way is up or down, what is true or false. Gaslighting has become a major buzzword. The short of it is that he makes you feel crazy for feeling the way you feel, like your interpretation of reality is the wrong one.

The most important quality to look for in a partner is someone who is willing to work on it. Even toxic relationships can be repaired if both people are committed to working on it. However, if he refuses to change or to try to understand your feelings and your needs, then there is nothing that can be done and your only choice is to leave.

What makes this so hard is that a guy with toxic qualities usually also has a lot of really good qualities, and we think if we try hard enough we can draw those positive qualities out even further and inspire him to change and be a better man. It rarely works that way; the only way people change is if they recognize there is a problem and they want to fix it. And no matter how many positive qualities he has, the only one that matters is a desire to make the relationship work. If he doesn't have that, then everything else is useless.

Another Thing...

But we also need to consider this...he's not always the only one to blame. If you're drawn to a toxic person, chances are, you're a little toxic yourself. The fact is, like attracts like. An emotionally healthy person will attract another emotionally healthy person. A toxic person will attract another toxic person. So ask yourself: *How am I contributing to this toxicity?*

Emotional maturity means taking responsibilities for ourselves, for our choices, for what we bring to the table. And sometimes, it takes two to create a toxic tango.

Remember this: Most of us have faulty ideas about love that originate in messages from mainstream media, our family life, or our first major relationship. (Sometimes it's a combination of all three!) True love isn't what most people think it is. It can be amazing and transformative, but only when both people are emotionally healthy and ready and willing to work on a relationship.

CHAPTER 3

What Prevents You from Finding Love

"You cannot make someone love you. You can only make yourself someone who can be loved." —*Derek Gamba*

Everyone will at some point find themselves asking this question: *Is there just no one out there for me, or am I the problem?* And people who perpetually feel dissatisfied in their relationships might wonder if the love they want actually exists, or if they're being delusional.

The fact is, finding the right person is a matter of *being* the right person. And you can be just as lonely (or even lonelier) in a relationship as you are when you're single. Most women spend a significant amount of time looking not only for love, but the right kind of love. They believe they'll know it when they see it (or feel it), but don't quite know how to get it.

In this chapter, we'll look at some of the most common stumbling blocks that prevent you from getting the love you want...some are sneakier than you think. This chapter isn't just for the single and dissatisfied; even if you're married you'll gain valuable insights into how to make your relationship even better.

The Real Reasons You Can't Find Love

Being single for a certain amount of time has its benefits. I personally experienced the most growth and self-awareness during my years as a single girl, and while there were some painful and lonely moments, they all led me to a place where I could break through some of my walls and do some necessary inner work.

At the same time, most people don't make it a goal to be single forever. Most of us want love and a partner to share our lives with, but we mistakenly go about trying to attain this thing we want so much in all the wrong ways. We continue to live life in the same way and hope that it will somehow lead to different results. We know that this doesn't really make any sense, and yet we continue to operate from our ingrained default setting.

Being single isn't a curse and being in a relationship isn't a cure-all. No matter what stage of life you're in, it's important to take a personal inventory—to look at the habits and choices that are helping you and the ones that are hurting you. It's not a matter of putting yourself out there more or of signing up for every dating site and side-swiping app—finding a truly amazing, healthy relationship is much more about being ready for such a relationship. It's about identifying faulty patterns and thought processes that may be blocking you from getting what you want.

To solve a problem, you need to understand it. So let's look at some of the main reasons why you might still be single when you don't want to be, and what you might unknowingly be doing to push love away. (And before we begin, I just want to say my goal isn't to shame or blame anyone. I'm not trying to place all the blame on you; I'm just going to discuss some of the most common areas I've seen women go wrong in their quest for love).

Reason #1
You're Too Needy

There's no faster way to repel a man than to *need* him. Wanting a man is not the same as *needing* one.

Neediness is a state of mind where you feel incomplete, or have an emotional void, and try to fill this empty space with a relationship or male validation. A lot of women confuse men's aversion to neediness with men's supposed aversion to commitment. But men aren't commitment-phobes (at least, the majority are not). A man will happily enter into a relationship with a woman who *sees* and *appreciates* him for exactly who he is. Conversely, a man will run far away from a woman who sees him as an opportunity to feel good about herself or fill some void.

A guy wants to feel *chosen* by a woman he had to *earn*. He doesn't want to feel like he's just filling a spot that could have easily gone to any other man with a pulse.

Solution: Neediness usually stems from a lack of self-esteem or sense of worth. You feel like something is missing within yourself or in your life and erroneously believe a relationship will be the cure. If you were unhappy before the relationship, you'll be unhappy in it. Instead of feeling sorry for yourself about being single, work on your relationship with yourself. Work on feeling your best and looking your best. When you are the best you that you can be, you won't be able to keep men away!

Reason #2
You're Too Picky

Most women are usually at one extreme or the other: desperate and willing to put up with anything, or too picky and unwilling to "settle" for anything less than their dream man.

In this day and age, we're saturated with unrealistic love sagas and have developed an idea of what love *should* be and not of what love *is*, as I discussed in chapter two. We're told that love conquers all, but in truth love alone does not make for a good and healthy relationship. (I mean, just about every divorced couple loved each other at some point.) We want to be swept off our feet and taken over by this all-consuming feeling of euphoria and harmony. If we're not feeling the intensity on the first date, we'll write the guy off and say there was no "spark."

Another problem is that most women have adopted a sometimes inflexible idea that it's "better to be alone than to settle." Taken to an extreme, this mindset causes many women to close themselves off to guys with amazing traits just because of some superficial flaw that rules him out as their dream guy. The longer you're single, the worse this can get because you might start telling yourself, "Well I've waited this long to find the one, I am *not* compromising on anything and deserve to get exactly what I want!"

One reason you operate at this high level of pickiness is that it's a defense mechanism—you reject before you are rejected. And this stems from fear. It's the fear of being hurt. The fear of being unlovable or unworthy. That is why working on your feelings of self worth is *crucial* (we will talk a lot more about this in chapter six).

Or maybe you want all the pain you've been through to mean something. Maybe you think there needs to be a reward for all the suffering in the form of the perfect man who will fulfill all your dreams.

It's OK to have standards and to have an idea of the kind of guy you want to be with, but it's also important to be a little flexible and realize that you might not get every single thing you want, and that doesn't mean you're settling.

Maybe you don't like his job, maybe you don't like the way he dresses, maybe you think his hobbies are lame. This all might be true, but it's important to realize that these things don't tell you *who he is*, and who he is might be a really wonderful, kind, caring person.

Solution: Make a list of three non-negotiable qualities you need in a man and three absolute dealbreakers. This does not include things like how much money he makes or how far back his hairline is. Money won't make for a happy marriage, and neither will a full head of hair, a chiseled jaw, or six-pack abs. Obviously you want to be attracted to your partner, but try not to get so caught up in the physical details. Also jot down three deal-breakers. This will help you gain clarity and perspective and take you away from relying on the long dating checklist you may have formed in your mind.

Next, when you go out with a guy and don't feel that all-consuming spark, don't write him off. Unless there was something that absolutely repulsed you about him, give him another shot. A lot of women are way too quick to dismiss a guy before really giving him a fair shot. I know more stories than I can even count of women who went on a few *meh* dates with the men they eventually married. Who knows where they would have ended up had they not given their future husbands another shot.

My husband doesn't have some of the main qualities that I used to swear up and down I couldn't live without. Through our relationship, I can now see how the type of guy I thought I wanted would have been a disaster when paired with my personality type. I, like most people, thought I knew myself way better than I actually did. Now every day I realize, with increasing awe, just how wrong I was about what I thought I needed, because I am with a person who couldn't be more suited for me.

When you open your mind just a bit, you might find yourself very pleasantly surprised!

Reason #3
You Haven't Worked On Yourself

The number one way to attract love is to make yourself into a vessel that can receive it.

A successful relationship comes down to two things: the right person at the right time. The first thing that's important to remember when it comes to relationships is that in general, like attracts like. That is, what you are or think you are is what you will attract.

If you don't value yourself, you will go for someone who doesn't treat you well, and you will be OK with it because he's just validating how you feel about yourself.

If you are emotionally unavailable, you will attract a guy who is emotionally unavailable. Now, you can want to be in a relationship and at the same time be unavailable in your own way. If you're afraid of getting hurt or feel like the guys you want always leave you, then you might subconsciously be putting up walls to protect yourself.

In order to attract a real relationship, you first need to make sure that you are in the right place emotionally. Make sure you want a relationship for the right reasons, not just to fill a void or make you feel better about yourself. You also need to develop a firm sense of who you are and learn how to be happy without a relationship.

It may seem like finding a great guy who likes you and sticks around, when others couldn't or wouldn't, will take the sting out of past rejection, but it doesn't work that way. If you're still holding onto hurt from the past, then it will spill over into your relationships in the present.

Good self-esteem attracts someone capable not only of healthy interactions but of loving you for who you are. If you're not sure of yourself inside, you'll seek validation outside.

Solution: I have a friend who asks herself every day, "Would I want to date me today?" I think it's a pretty amazing exercise and will help you realize where you're falling short and what you need to work on.

If you want an emotionally healthy, confident, stable guy, then you need to make sure you mirror those qualities at the same level. I mean, why would a guy like that want to be with someone who is an insecure emotional mess? If you want that kind of guy, you need to be that kind of girl.

As soon as you're in that place where you are your best self and you mirror the qualities you want, you'll notice an instant change in your love life; you'll find that you can easily get the kind of guy and the kind of relationship you've always wanted. This path will be different for everyone, but try as best you can to discover the best path for you.

Reason #4
You Want Emotionally Unavailable Guys

One of the biggest obstacles standing in your way and stopping you from having the relationship you want is wanting the guys who don't want you. It's a ubiquitous phenomenon. Every day my inbox gets flooded with questions from women plotting and strategizing to capture a man who does not seem to want to be captured...at least not by her.

I am an expert on the subject because for far too many years the only guys who held any sort of intrigue for me were the ones I couldn't quite have. And the ones who were head over heels in love with me and willing to do anything for me? Blech, I didn't want them. I wanted to want them and everything they offered, but I just didn't. And the heart wants what the heart wants, right?

Before I started dating my husband, I dated a guy I'll call Kevin. Kevin was yet another classic case of the type of guy I just couldn't seem to resist. He was charming, charismatic, confident, fun, and always slightly beyond my grasp. He also had some deep-rooted emotional problems to deal with and some major commitment issues.

He was a classic "damage case," a guy who has a lot of potential hidden under a pile of issues. The "bad boy" who needs to be saved. And like many women, I wanted to be his healer, to be the woman who inspired him to break through his walls and finally commit.

He liked me...but nothing ever really came of it. We went on a few dates, and then he told me he didn't think it would work out between us. But then we would see each other, and he would lock in on me and things would start up again. But then he would be gone. But then he would be back, and this time it would feel like it was *our time*. But he's gone again. And it keeps happening, ripping me to shreds a little more each time he left.

And the sad and slightly embarrassing fact is, I spent over a year hung up on this guy who dumped me after a few dates. I was like a hungry puppy panting at his feet, hoping he would finally choose me. Anytime it seemed like maybe he was changing his mind, maybe he was reciprocating, the rug would be ripped right out from under me once again.

Damage cases are like a pair of super sexy shoes that are brutally uncomfortable. When you look at them they're amazing—they're beautiful and sexy and you have to have them. But when you wear them you're in agony. Then you take them off and experience euphoric relief, the most incredible feeling. But this feeling doesn't come from gaining something positive, it comes from removing something negative—pain. This experience is the same as dating an unavailable guy.

He seems to be everything you want, so enticing you can't resist him. But when you have him, you just feel pain and discomfort. Your stomach is in knots as you wait for the next text, or for a sign that he truly cares. Then he gives you some sort of indication that he does, and you're ecstatic; you feel a rush of euphoria. But then he pulls back again and you're back in those unbearable shoes. Then he comes back, and relief. And on and on it goes.

When I was younger I kept chasing the high of removing those painful shoes. And I thought if only X would happen, then I would have that taking-shoes-off feeling forever. As I got older, I realized I didn't want to be on this roller coaster ride anymore. I decided that a comfortable pair of shoes that gave me the support I needed and a steady feeling of ease was much better than a sporadic shocking jolt of relief.

Kevin was the catalyst for this realization. It had been a while since I'd chased after a damage case, and I thought I'd nipped that problem in the bud until he came along and got me all twisted like a pretzel. It was devastating on many levels, especially to my ego! I mean, I was supposed to know better at that point—I was a relationship expert for crying out loud!

Solution: After a series of letdowns, of high hopes and thinking things would be different, followed by crushing disappointment and feeling like a fool for once again thinking the same story would have a different ending, I made a firm resolution to end this cycle for good. To make a lasting change that would lead me to the kind of love and relationship I really wanted. I was going to finally figure out why I kept going after the guys who didn't want me.

After being crushed by Kevin yet again, I decided to sit down and ask myself some really tough questions. What was I getting out of this relationship? Why was I so drawn to him even though I objectively knew he wouldn't be a good long-term partner? What had he even given to me? I did a lot for him, but what had he ever actually done to show me he cared? (The answer was nothing.)

I was getting nothing out of the relationship except for quick shots of temporary validation whenever he seemed to reciprocate my interest, and that is just so very sad. And then I realized that I am not the kind of woman who needs that sort of thing anymore. Maybe I did when I was younger, but I'm not that girl anymore, and I don't need to repeat history in order to subconsciously mend some old wounds.

Next I looked at why I kept going back to Kevin even though it was clear that the relationship was a dead end. I thought long and hard about what I was getting from him that kept drawing me back in, and the answer went beyond validation. I realized that with Kevin, I felt less alone and maybe a little understood. Like me, he was a little lost and hurt, and that made me feel better in my own world of lost and hurt.

I also considered what I was giving to the relationship (if you could even call it that) and why. Why was I so invested in solving his issues? Why was I so wrapped up in getting inside his head? The reason, I believe, is that getting lost in his drama was an escape from dealing with my own. I had a reprieve from my own life and my own issues, one of which was why I was so drawn to damage cases like Kevin! I felt like I had a mission and a purpose, and that felt kind of nice...at least for a little while.

Once I saw the situation for what it was, it lost all appeal for me. Instead of feeling sorry for myself because I couldn't get him to commit in the way I wanted, I felt sorry for him for having so many issues that prevented him from committing to a great woman he had right in front of him.

Soon after I processed all of this and healed, I started dating my now husband. On our first date I could tell by the way he was looking at me that he was already smitten and it was clear that he was on the same page as me, he wanted what I wanted, and everything was just aligned. I was ecstatic, as one is at the beginning of an amazing relationship, but it wasn't the terrifying sort of exhilaration of feeling that this could all end at any moment. It was a stable sort of excitement.

There was no hunt, no chase, no guessing games. I knew how he felt; I didn't even have to ask, it was just so obvious. And I knew I was cured from my damage case addiction because the fact that he wanted me didn't turn me off. Instead it made him even more appealing.

(And in case you're wondering, Kevin is still as single and afraid of commitment as ever...no hard feelings though, I still run into him here and there, and we're friendly. I can't help but laugh to myself when I think about all the inner turmoil he caused... although he was also the catalyst that got me emotionally ready to be in a relationship with my husband, so maybe I owe him a thank you!)

Remember, damage cases are a waste of time and energy. Wanting a guy who doesn't want you is a tragedy. Time is a precious thing to waste, so get to work and undo the faulty wiring that leads you to the guys who can't appreciate you.

More than anything else, the path that leads to lasting love involves making yourself a vessel to receive love. If you only want guys who can't want you back then you are blocked, so make the decision, right here and now, to push yourself to break free and clear away all the obstacles preventing you from getting what you truly want.

Reason #5
Faulty Filter Systems

A bad filter system sets you up for failure before your relationship has a chance to get off the ground, if you even get that far.

Everyone has a certain ingrained filter system. This system is partially due to genetic wiring, but it is largely shaped by our experiences. This filter system is often based on our interests, desires, and fears. For instance, if you are afraid of rejection, all you'll pick up on is being rejected. A hundred people can tell you how great and wonderful you are, but it won't sink in. All that will stand out to you is the one person who didn't seem to be interested in you.

If you put ten people in a room and have them listen to a class and then ask them at the end what the class was about, you'll get ten different answers. We hone in on things that appeal to us and serve our interests in some way and ignore the rest. And what is focused on and what is ignored varies from one person to the next.

So how does this affect your relationships?

Your reality is created in large part by your filter system. If you believe that the guys you want will never want you, you will find a justification for this fear even if it's far from the case. Once you come to expect the behavior, you create a self-fulfilling prophecy.

Whether consciously or not, you will start to behave in a way that turns men off (this can be *very* subtle and might not come across in anything you say or do), thus feeding into your original fear. If you are afraid your boyfriend will never commit in the way you want him to, you will ignore all signs of his commitment and will only focus on the signs that he doesn't want to commit.

Your fear will manifest itself in behavior like clinging more tightly to the relationship or being on guard for its inevitable end, which will, in turn, cause the relationship to unravel. I'm not talking about situations where a guy clearly won't commit, like a guy not calling you his girlfriend after an extended period of time. I'm talking about more subtle signs.

If you believe you're unattractive, you will dismiss everyone who compliments your appearance and will write it off as them just being nice. When someone says something that implies they don't find you attractive, you'll grab hold of it and will use it as proof of your original belief.

We have an innate need to justify our thought patterns, even if these patterns don't serve us in a positive way.

Want proof? Close your eyes and pick a color. Visualize the color in your mind, picture items that are that color, see yourself dressed in that color, think about the emotions that color evokes. Spend about 30 seconds to a minute doing this and then open your eyes, what's the first thing you saw? I guarantee it will be that color unless you did this in an all-white room. If we dwell on something, even for under a minute, our mind becomes programmed to pick it up.

We're all wired to look at the world in subjective ways. Reality is not objective; it is shaped by both what happens to us and how we interpret the things that happen to us. Changing the way you think can literally change your life. It takes practice, patience, and mindfulness but when you commit yourself to it you will create a new reality for yourself.

Solution: In order to have more success in love and relationships, you need to adjust your filter system so that you see the good all around you. You need to be able to appreciate and acknowledge the goodness that is in you and in your relationship. If you let your fears run the show, you will set yourself up for sabotage.

First, you need to weed out faulty thought patterns. Anytime a negative thought pops into your mind (*I'll never find a boyfriend...I'm going to end up alone...Men always leave me*), pluck it out and tell yourself the opposite. This applies not only to relationships, but it also applies and can be used to enhance all areas of your life. Our thoughts have a huge impact on the way we feel, and since we can control what we think our thoughts are a very powerful tool once we start using them.

I am also a big fan of keeping a gratitude journal. Every day, jot down 1-2 things you're grateful for (and pick different things every day). This will retrain your brain to focus on the good. Maybe it sounds cheesy, but I've done this exercise and I recommend it to readers all the time, and the results are truly transformative.

Reason #6
The Ex Factor

Most of us are unaware of all the ways our past can bleed into our present—and even our future—if left unchecked.

I have been hurt a lot over the years, for which I am thankful. The pain has served me well in that it's given me invaluable insights into relationships (and provided me with a plethora of content to write about!), but I also came to a point where I realized the extent to which I never fully processed and let go of some of that toxic baggage.

They say time heals all wounds, but I find that is only partially true. Time makes you forget or it makes the memories more distant, but it doesn't automatically heal the wounds left behind. Healing from a devastating breakup (or any traumatic event) isn't a passive process; it is something you need to actively work on.

A relationship is going to unfold in only one of two ways: it will either last forever or it will fall apart. In order to get the relationship that lasts, you have to come to terms with all the ones that didn't.

When I first started dating my husband, even though I felt very sure about his intentions I had a really tough time fully trusting him and the relationship. More importantly, I had a hard time trusting myself and my own judgment. Even though I knew my fears had absolutely nothing to do with him, I couldn't get past them.

I knew these feelings were coming from me because he did nothing to make me think he was anything other than fully committed to making the relationship work. But sometimes seemingly small, innocent things would trigger my fears and insecurities. For example, anytime he would try to reassure me by saying "I'm not going anywhere," I would feel my guard reflexively come up and I would become a bit more distant, withdrawn, and uneasy. He was understandably hurt by this and thought I didn't believe him or didn't trust him, but that wasn't it.

With a little self-reflection I was able to pinpoint exactly why it was happening. You see, one of my exes used to say that line anytime my insecurities would flare up. And I believed him. Those words gave me an instant feeling of calm and security (it never lasted long because it wasn't the right relationship at all), but it did assuage my fears temporarily. Even though the relationship was far from ideal, I believed he would never leave. I believed he couldn't live without me, just as I couldn't possibly live without him or fathom a world without him in it.

The relationship had its ups and downs...and even though the downs were becoming more frequent and long lasting, I believed we would power through it. I believed we were in it together and would make it work. But we didn't. Instead, my greatest fear became a reality; he left me for someone else and showered her with all the love he had been incapable of giving me.

Saying I was devastated doesn't do justice to the state I was in. Rather than process what had happened, I partied like there was no tomorrow. I made sure to leave no open space for the pain to slip in. I was going, going, going, no time to stop. No time to think, or worst of all, feel.

In the years that followed, I became hardened and my once open heart was now unable to feel anything for any man I dated. One by one they would fall hard for me, but I would feel nothing. There were a few guys who managed to stir something inside of me, and I would inexplicably fall hard and fast. My stomach would be in knots waiting for the next text, I would endlessly analyze everything he did to determine whether or not he liked me, I would constantly plan and plot what I would say and do to win him over. But nothing ever came from those "relationships"—save for me being left devastated—because the only guys who could get me to feel anything were the emotionally unavailable ones.

My objective mind couldn't see this, though, because my attraction to these guys was rooted in my subconscious. My last relationship had instilled a belief in me that I was unworthy of love, that I would never get the guy I wanted, that no man would love the real me. So, I sought out guys who weren't in a place to love anyone, really, and was proven right time and time again. That's the thing about the subconscious, it always seeks validation, even if it's in the form of a painful reality.

What happened to me is something that happens to many people after a toxic relationship and crushing breakup: I internalized faulty beliefs about myself and never challenged them.

Almost a decade after the relationship that broke me, I realized just how deep the scars were. I realized I had adopted a set of beliefs about myself that was sabotaging my efforts to find the love I'd always wanted. So I decided to dig deep into the darkness to purge these beliefs. I looked at that relationship through an objective lens and realized the way it had unfolded had absolutely nothing to do with who I really am.

At the time, I thought he'd left me because I wasn't good enough... because I was unlovable...because I was unworthy. I also stopped trusting my own judgment. I had stayed with him even though he was clearly bad for me. I had trusted him based on the few words of assurance he would provide when I was feeling insecure, and ignored all the glaring red flags. How could I trust myself not to make the same mistake again? As a result, I became a woman who believed she couldn't trust her instincts, who couldn't trust men, who couldn't open up and be vulnerable and let anyone else in.

Good relationships bring all your unresolved issues to the surface. Even though I had done a lot of internal work before I started dating my husband, there was a lot more that needed to be done. It started with realizing that this relationship is the complete opposite of the last one, and I am a completely different person now, so it is absurd to think I would repeat the same mistakes.

The subconscious doesn't operate from a place of reason and logic, it operates from a place of emotion. What I needed to internalize was that even though certain things felt real (like that he was going to just leave me out of the blue one day, and I needed to be on guard at all times lest I miss some warning sign), they were not reality. Feelings aren't facts, and when you look at a situation objectively, you often see just how silly and unfounded your beliefs truly are.

Once I realized what was happening, I was able to challenge some of those old faulty beliefs and replace them with newer, happier truths. I was able to finally relax and let love in. My guy noticed the change immediately, and our relationship improved drastically.

Solution: If you've been hurt in the past, try to see if you can identify any old wounds you're still carrying around with you. Think about how you interpreted the situation at the time and see if you can spot any faulty beliefs about yourself that may have developed. Then do whatever you need to in order to correct those. It isn't always easy, but it is so worth it.

But let's talk a little more about the ex factor...

The Real Reasons You're Still Hung Up On Your Ex

No matter how toxic (and pointless) it is to continue pining for an ex, most women have a near impossible time letting go and moving forward. It's a big problem and a big topic, and I want to dive in a little deeper and look at the real reasons women have such a hard time letting go.

Let's say you had a job where you felt perpetually stressed, anxious, and miserable. You put in all you could, even if it came at the expense of your ego and sometimes, your sanity. And let's say you got fired from that job.

Yes, being unemployed is scary so at first you'd feel upset and worried, but you would also probably feel relieved. You'd realize it was for the best and would be thankful that you were now free to find a job better suited to you, one where you would feel valued and appreciated. You wouldn't spend sleepless nights pining for that old job, wondering what went wrong and what else you could have done. You'd realize, with perfect clarity, that it wasn't the right place for you.

Now let's say you're in a relationship where you feel perpetually stressed, anxious, worried, and miserable. You put everything you have into making it work. You give it your all, even at the expense of your dignity and emotional well-being. You put up a good fight, but it's not enough and he breaks up with you. You were miserable with him, and now you're even more miserable without him. You spend months, maybe even years, pining away.

Unfortunately, a relationship is hard to view through the same objective lens as a job. With relationships, it's not just our emotions that get involved, it's our egos, our past pain, our childhood traumas, our insecurities, our fears. Everything gets activated, and when the bomb detonates it can take months or years to clear away the wreckage.

As a result, when a relationship ends it's not just the other person that's missing; a lot of pieces of yourself also need to be retrieved. Many people make the mistake of thinking that the reason they're so sad after a breakup is because they genuinely miss their former partner. This is true to an extent, but it's far from the whole picture. The pain we feel comes from several sources, and most have nothing to do with the ex himself.

Here are the *real* reasons it's so hard to get over him:

Reason #1
You Think You'll Never Find Anyone As Amazing As Him

This is the biggest breakup myth of all and the reason most people find it so hard to get over their first love. They cling to the belief that since they never experienced anything like that before, they never will again.

You convince yourself that no other man on the planet has the same qualities as him and thus you have two choices: get him back or settle for someone who will never measure up. I hope you can recognize the absurdity of this!

Will you meet someone else exactly like him? No, because no two people are exactly alike. But more importantly, you wouldn't want to—you and he broke up, proving that someone exactly like him is exactly what you *don't* need. You won't find someone with his exact qualities; you will find someone even better and more compatible with you.

Reason #2
You Sold Yourself Out

In unhealthy relationships, we will often "sell ourselves out" or demean ourselves in an effort to make it work. It is the same as letting him cross your boundaries. It means accepting behavior that you would otherwise consider unacceptable, or attempting to be someone you're not. Maybe you don't speak up anymore, maybe you aren't the same bubbly, confident person you once were, or maybe you unquestioningly put him and his needs above your own.

The emotional devastation you feel after a breakup is usually proportional to the extent you sold yourself out. When these relationships end, you will often feel like a piece of you is missing, like you aren't whole. It's a miserable, almost sickening feeling. You might feel like getting him back is the only cure, but it's not. You need to reclaim the pieces of yourself that you lost.

What you need to do is look at yourself and really try to determine why you accepted such poor treatment for so long, and what steps you can take to avoid getting into a situation like this again.

You stayed for a reason, you were getting something out of being there. What was it? And what steps can you take to avoid being in that situation again?

Reason #3
You Miss The Way He Made You F*eel*

Most of the time, it's not the guy you're missing...it's the feelings you experienced when you were with him. You miss the intimacy, the closeness, the feeling of being desired and admired. You miss the way he made you feel more than who he actually is. And the reason you can't move on is that you've attached those needs onto a person...and your mind tricks you into believing you will never have those things again unless you get him back.

There is almost always a period of withdrawal after an important element of your life is gone. Whether it's your decision to cut him out of your life or not, there will suddenly be a void, and you may feel unbalanced as you try to cope without the thing that was once there to fuel you. It's like quitting coffee or cigarettes. At first you think you'll never be able to make it through the day without your "fix." It will definitely be hard at first, but when you push past the initial discomfort, you'll find you can function just as well or even better!

Whenever you catch yourself missing him and pining for him, stop and ask yourself: **What do I really miss?**

Maybe the answer is: I miss the connection we shared.

Now you're going to turn it around and use that as a data point about yourself: I am someone who craves connection. When you do this, you separate the need from the person and this will make it easier to move on.

Once you've gathered the data point, ask yourself: *What can I do today to increase my feelings of connection?*

Maybe you reach out to close friends or family. Or maybe you do something that connects you to yourself, to your essence.

Focus on rebuilding your life in a way that makes you feel fulfilled and content with who you are. You probably relied on him to give you a feeling of worth, and now it's time to take ownership and give yourself that feeling.

Reason #4
You Lost Yourself

A boyfriend can often quickly go from being a part of your life to being your *entire* life. You stop seeing your friends as much, doing hobbies you enjoy, pursuing your passions. You want to spend every free moment with him and can't pry yourself away. It feels like he's your everything...because he is! And when "everything" leaves, you're left with nothing. You feel empty, like a piece of you is missing.

When you lose yourself in a relationship, your entire sense of self-worth relies on the relationship. You need him to feed your ego and if you don't get enough fuel, you feel a gaping emptiness. So of course you are an absolute distraught mess when the relationship ends. He didn't just leave, he took your entire self-worth with him.

The fact is, a lot of pieces of you are missing and you need to find them; he isn't the final magical puzzle piece that can complete you. The process of finding those lost pieces of yourself starts with rebuilding your life and making it full and balanced without him. When you drop other elements of your life and have your guy fill that space, you will have a huge hole once he leaves you. Realize that this hole exists not because he was the other half of your soul, but because you threw many important elements of your life overboard.

Reason #5
You Took It Too Personally

A lot of the time, the pain we feel after a breakup is really the throb of a severely bruised ego. Rejection hurts. Even if it's only because of incompatibility, it can still sting and make you feel like you're somehow not good enough. But sometimes two people just aren't a match, it's as simple as that. Sometimes both people can see this with perfect clarity, while sometimes only one person does.

Being single can be tough and dating can be exhausting, but neither of these options is as bad as being stuck in an unhealthy relationship. Everyone has things they want to give to and get from a relationship. If what you give is what the other person can receive, and vice versa, then it's a match. If not, then it doesn't mean either of you is bad or damaged or not good enough, it just means you're not a match, and that's OK.

Try not to take it too personally and instead realize that while this might not have been the right relationship for you, the next one very well might be, so your best bet is to mentally and emotionally move past this relationship so you can open the door for someone even better to walk through.

As I mentioned in the introduction of this book, a lot of the time the pain we feel is because of the story we tell ourselves about what happened. After a breakup, a lot of women tell themselves it's because he never truly cared. She may feel betrayed, maybe by him or maybe by her own mind, for thinking reality was one way when really it was another. But here is the thing: two things can be true at the same time.

It can be true that he loved you with all his heart...he just didn't see a future with you. The fact that he didn't see a future with you *does not* necessarily mean he was stringing you along this entire time and that you've been played.

Our minds operate in black and white terms, we look at a straight cause and effect relationship. If it didn't work out...it must mean he never loved me. But two seemingly opposing things can be true at the same time. It can be true that it didn't work out...but he also did and does truly love you!

The point is: don't create a story around this to paint yourself in a negative light (*I'm unworthy...I'm unlovable...I'll end up alone...*). And don't lash out against all men (T*hey're all narcissists...They all lie...they will all break your heart),* because none of these things are true and it simply doesn't help you to think in these terms. Conversely, it will only hurt you and prevent you from getting what you really want.

Try to see it as a lesson learned, rather than a reflection of who you are as a person. Having a growth mindset is what will arm you against the pain of rejection and will just make every challenge you face in life less daunting.

A study called "Changes in Self-Definition Impede Recovery from Rejection" published in the *Personality and Social Psychology Bulletin* by Carol Dweck and Lauren Howe[1] examined why some people move on from rejection swiftly and other stay stuck mired in the pain for months or years. They found that participants with a fixed or static mindset (assuming your character, intelligence, and creative ability are static givens and can't change in any meaningful way) let the romantic rejection linger. They saw rejection as being a reflection of who they are which caused them to be more guarded in future relationships.

Conversely, participants with a growth mindset (thriving on challenge and seeing failure as an opportunity for growth), were able to let go even though they too were hurt by the rejection and were able to see a bright future for themselves.

The findings were clear: taking rejection personally and thinking it means something about you will keep you stuck in that pain and you will bring it into your future.

Reason #6
You're Idealizing The Past

Most people seem to develop selective amnesia after a relationship ends whereby they only remember the good times and completely ignore everything that went on the rest of the time. I'm sure you shared plenty of good times and happy memories, but that's not all that went on, or the relationship wouldn't have ended.

Be real with yourself and honest about the relationship. Remind yourself of the reasons why it *didn't* work, instead of going over what you could have or should have done differently in order to *make* it work. Chances are, it would have ended no matter what you did differently.

Breakups don't happen because of small details, they occur because the two individuals in their entirety simply weren't a match. No amount of ruminating will change this so it's best to just accept it and move forward.

A breakup can feel almost like a death...and it kind of is. It's the death of potential, the death of all the possibilities that could have been. In the beginning you were so full of hope and optimism, two of the most uplifting and exhilarating feelings there are. And now you're having a hard time parting with those feelings and everything you'd hoped for, a hard time accepting that while what you and he shared was good, it wasn't good enough. But it's OK. Not every relationship is meant to stand the test of time so don't think of it as the end of something, think of it as just the beginning of your journey towards finding the right one.

When You're Too Intimidating

There is a difference between being intimidating and intimidating someone away. If you feel like the guys you want are always intimidated by you then I can relate because I was in this boat. I mean I made a career writing about men for a living and writing about my relationships. When guys would date me, they would be intimidated by it!

It's very easy to write off being unlucky in love by saying, "He was just intimidated by me." This takes the blame off you and actually is a way to make you feel better about yourself because you were just too amazing for him. But then we have to go back to one of Tai's famous lines in Clueless—"If I'm too good for him, then how come I'm not with him?"

Well, it may be because you're tapping into the wrong energy and presenting yourself in the wrong light.

No, this doesn't mean you need to put on a facade or change who you are to attract the person you want. You just need to be conscious of which energy you're tapping into and at what point.

OK, first thing, a lot of the time, people who define themselves as alpha are just masquerading their insecurities as admirable traits. They define themselves as strong and independent and alpha. And all that's great...but they use it to keep people out. They use it as armor. They may struggle with opening up, with being vulnerable, with letting people in...and they reason it's because they are just *too* self-sufficient and don't need anyone. But sometimes, these attributes are rooted in fear. They are afraid to get too close, afraid to rely on someone else.

But yet, they still want to form a connection. They crave that intimacy but feel they are just too intimidating to ever have it.

So are you truly alpha, or are you putting up a certain front because it's easier than confronting what lies beneath?

Maybe you're just too scared to let people in because you've been hurt in the past. Maybe you just don't trust people because you've been let down too many times.

So first, be honest about what's making you come across as so intimidating.

Connect With Him As A Person

A lot of us relate to people as extensions of ourselves. We think in terms of what they reflect back to us—they only exist in terms of how they see us. Did he think I was nice? Pretty? Polite? Smart?

We do this with romantic prospects as well as strangers. You order a coffee at Starbucks and the barista has an angry face on and you wonder, "Did she think I was rude? Was my order too intricate? Does she think I'm a mean person?" You see her scowl as a reflection of you when really, she's probably having a bad day because she's a separate entity from you with her own life and not every facial expression someone makes is about us!

Stop relating to a man (or to people in general!) as an extension of you, meaning, if he is impressed by me, I'm impressive! Instead relate to him as another human being with his own story, his own world, his own issues.

Stop Planning And Analyzing

Now this comes in a few forms. Some women stress because of insecurities—they stress because they are protecting themselves from getting hurt because deep down they believe getting hurt is inevitable.

Some women are just alpha personalities and they get caught up in analyzing every detail, micromanaging, and planning a future with a guy when they're five minutes into the first date.

I have a friend who is a classic example of this. She has a super successful career as an event planner. Being so detail oriented and forward-thinking helped her get where she is in her career, but using the same strategies in her love life was causing problems.

After going on a first date with a guy she really liked, she called me and said, "Well he's great and all, but he's getting started with a new business venture, so that means he won't be able to financially provide for a while which means I would have to be the breadwinner. And I'm fine with that, but I'm already in my mid 30s and I want to have kids soon, but how will we work our finances out? So I'll have to wait until he's in a more stable financial position before we have kids, but his new job is based in the city and he said this is where he needs to be, but I really want to move to the suburbs when I have a kid..." and on and on.

Girl, *woah woah woah*! You went on one date with this guy and you're already budgeting for a house in the suburbs and preschools for kids that don't exist yet?!

This is not a good energy to be around. This is an intimidating energy to be around because he doesn't feel like you're connecting or relating to him, he feels like you're sizing him up, and no one likes that feeling.

It feels like a job interview. And no one likes being at a job interview; it's something we endure because we have to.

Let's think about this point a little more. At a job interview, I'm sure you can feel it when the interviewer is looking for reasons *to* hire you, as opposed to reasons not to. We feel it. And when we feel like we're being sized up and judged, we want to run away and get out of there as quickly as possible.

This also leads to another point. The sizing him up mentality. A lot of women have mental checklists of what we think we want, and we size a guy up to see if he fits the bill. We don't connect with what is, we are looking at how well he aligns with the type of person we think we should be with.

Again, this sends out an intimidating energy. Think about times in your life when someone was judging you and you felt it; it doesn't feel so good!

Instead of asking do I want to marry this person, just ask, do I want to go on another date with this person?

Try to just be present and in the moment with no strategy or game plan.

Don't Do All The Work

Another issue my friend had was she would do *all* the work. She would plan the dates, she would initiate the plans, she was in charge. Again, great in the workplace, not great in the dating space!

Yes, make plans, suggest date ideas, but don't do all the work.

We come to invest when we *give* to someone else. That is how love is formed. If you're doing everything—you're initiating all the plans, you're texting first, you're coming up with creative dates, you're filling every silence and always thinking of something interesting and clever to say—then there is no room for him to invest and you will be the only one with any stake in this relationship.

Lead With Softness

You don't need to make yourself small, but it will help you to make yourself a little more soft. Be warm, be approachable, be friendly, be easygoing.

This isn't just about attracting a man. This is just a more attractive energy in general, this makes you more attractive to everyone. This is what makes you magnetic and makes people want to be around you and align themselves with you.

Don't seek to impress, seek to connect.

And above all, do what is authentic to you. Don't ever mold yourself to be what someone else wants. You can lead with softness while still being your true, alpha self. You just want him to see who your true self really is and that's hard to do when you're being too dominant.

The Secret To Getting Love That Lasts

Here is an Instagram-able quote for you to always keep in mind: *It's not about finding the right person, it's about being the right person.*

Years ago, I attended a friend's wedding, and it was a very happy occasion not just because weddings are always happy occasions, but because this friend in particular went through a *lot* in the love department. From coming home one day and finding her live-in boyfriend of several years in bed with another woman to getting dumped out of the blue by the first guy she really saw a future with after that cheating boyfriend, to going out with one guy after the next after the next after the next and getting nowhere.

Seeing how happy she was and how amazing she and her now husband are together was really touching and inspiring. The day before the wedding, she and I got to talking and I asked her how she knew he was the one. She replied, "I knew it on our second date. I just felt like my absolute best self around him." This is one extremely important point about relationships, one that most people overlook.

Before meeting her husband, my friend had dated a string of really incredible, high-quality guys. The pattern was that they would go out on a few dates (maybe an average of 3-5) and one after the next would pull the plug and end it.

At first she was really hurt, but eventually she just got frustrated and wanted to know why this kept happening. So she decided to be bold and find out exactly why these guys dumped her.

If she had a friend in common with the guy, she would send that person to investigate. If not, she would call the guy up and say in a very casual and non-confrontational way, "I want to ask you something honestly...I thought we had a good thing and I'm just curious to know why you didn't want to continue dating. I've been noticing a pattern in my life of this happening and I'm starting to think maybe it's me and would really appreciate your insights."

Because she was coming from a sincere place, she got honest answers. And pretty much every guy gave her the same answer. They all felt she was a bit too muted emotionally and they couldn't really connect with her because of it.

Once she knew the problem, she went on a mission to correct it. She bought books, attended seminars, and started seeing a therapist to work through some of her issues that she thought might be causing this block. She stopped serial dating and decided to spend some time focusing exclusively on her relationship with herself.

After a few months of hard internal work, she met the man who is now her husband.

"The one thing I wish I'd realized sooner is how important it is to work on yourself," she told me. "You really should write about this and tell your readers!"

I've mentioned the importance of working on yourself already in this book (and don't worry, we'll keep talking about it in much greater depth as we go on!), but this is probably my favorite relationship success story so I had to share it to really hammer in the point.

The part I found the most interesting about this story is how a connection was instantly formed when my friend met her husband. I wonder if this would have been the case had she not worked on herself and still been emotionally closed off.

Personal development is a lifetime commitment. We should never, ever, stop trying to be our best versions of ourselves or stop working on improving our weak points. It's not just about getting a guy, it's about living a life that is better and more fulfilling all around.

Having an amazing guy in your life is a wonderful thing that can certainly add to your happiness, but it won't ever be the sole source of happiness in your life. Happiness is an internal state that takes time and work. It isn't something that just happens; it won't just show up at your door one day.

To get the love you want, focus on building a solid foundation of self-love. Focus on working on yourself and pushing past those walls that close you off and hold you back. Feelings are scary and being vulnerable can be downright terrifying, but confronting these feelings head on is better than living your life behind Plexiglas.

What's that like? It's like sitting inside a coffee shop looking out the window at the New York City streets. You feel like you get a sense of what's going on out there, but you aren't feeling the wind in your face, you're not smelling the street meat, you aren't immersed in the hustle and bustle, you aren't filled with that pulsing energy. You are a spectator, not a participant. You're close, but not close enough to be in it. That's what happens when you hold yourself back, when you put up a plastic wall, when you live with the fears from your past, and when you take solace in the wall rather than actively working on ripping it down.

Instead of living behind it, say thank you to the wall. It served its purpose but you don't need it anymore. You are free to let yourself feel and be present and be open, and you are free to remove any obstacles holding you back.

Remember this: Being single has its benefits, but if you want to settle down you need to take a good hard look at what might be holding you back...and make a concerted effort to deal with it!

CHAPTER 4

The Dead-End Relationship

"A dead end can never be a one-way street; you can always turn around and take another road." —*Bo Bennett*

Settling for what you don't want is the surest way to *not* get what you do want. Feminine energy is a manifestor, we take potential and actualize it, and this can be a beautiful thing. The downside is a lot of women end up *dating* potential. She may stick it out with a man who won't or can't give her what she wants because of how much potential there is. She reasons that maybe if she sticks it out long enough...maybe once he's more settled in his job...maybe once his depression lifts...maybe when the busy season at his job is over...maybe when the divorce is finalized...maybe once he sees how perfect they would be together...maybe he just needs more time, more patience, more love. She can maybe her way into a dead-end relationship that goes on for months or years or decades!

It's a huge waste of time and energy, and it really does a number on your sense of self.

Signs He'll Never Commit

Is he serious about me? Does he really like me? Will he ever commit to me?

Trust me, I've experienced those gut-twisting feelings, the ones that leave you with a constant sense of impending doom in the pit of your stomach causing you to question everything, including yourself.

It's understandable. There is a lot at stake when you put your heart on the line and you can end up wasting months, or years, of your life on a man who never intended to keep you around for the long haul. And the aftermath of these situations is never pretty.

So what can we do to spare ourselves the time, energy, and heartbreak that goes into determining how a man feels?

After giving this topic a lot of thought and interviewing countless guys, I've uncovered five telltale signs that he isn't going to commit to you now or ever.

1. You Don't Know Anything Real About Him

You can talk to someone for hours and hours every day and not know anything real about him. You might know details about his life, but you don't know who he really is, his real and true self that exists beneath all the superficial fluff.

I'll use myself as an example.

Let's say I was out with a guy and he asked me what I did for a living. My basic answer would be that I write about relationships. That's something that I tell anyone I meet who asks me what I do.

Now if they ask why I chose this as a profession, I'd say that I like it, it's fun, and I'm good at it.

Now let's go a layer deeper. Why do I write about relationships? Well, I studied psychology in college and I've always been interested in human behavior and fascinated by the dynamics of relationships.

And now a level deeper...

I write about relationships because I want to help people, and I have a vested interest in helping girls heal from heartbreak.

And now a level deeper...

I've been hurt by men in my life—I've really had my heart annihilated—and writing about relationships is cathartic. It has helped me heal from my own pain, and I've been able to help a lot of other women in the process.

Anyone can know I write about relationships, but when talking about *why* I do, there are many levels that go far beyond the first superficial answer.

I used this example to illustrate a larger point: there is knowing someone, and there is *knowing* someone.

When a guy opens up to you, when he shares his dreams, his fears, his hopes, his wishes, his motivations, etc., he is investing in you. By investing in you, he is committing himself to you. Maybe you're not official, maybe you haven't said "I Love You," maybe he isn't proposing, but he's still committed.

We don't share ourselves with just anyone. Most of us have been burned badly enough in our lives to learn to be selective about the people we open up to.

Opening ourselves up comes with big risks. We become vulnerable and we also feel closer and more connected to the person we've revealed ourselves to.

If a guy doesn't share his true self with you, if he won't let you see who he is at his core, the chances are high that he's not in it for the long haul and doesn't see a future with you. Or maybe he has serious commitment issues and just can't open up, and while that is very sad for him, it's not really your job to fix him. And unfortunately, that's what most women do and the consequences are devastating.

If you're really unsure about whether or not a guy is serious about you, take a look at the things you know about him and ask yourself if you *really* know who he is. Don't panic if you don't know the real stuff yet—we'll talk about how to create a deep emotional connection a little later!

2. He Disappears For Days Or Weeks At A Time, Then Acts Like It's No Big Deal

If a guy truly cares about you, he will want to make room for you in his life. Even if he has a lot going on and won't be available for a few days, he'll send a text or message to let you know he's thinking about you.

If he takes vacations from the relationship with no warning it means he isn't worried about losing you, and this is never a good sign. If a guy knows for certain that you'll always be there waiting in the wings, no matter how badly he behaves, he won't respect you and he definitely won't want to commit to you—why should he when he knows he doesn't have to? There would be absolutely no benefit for him.

His disappearing acts serve more as a way to let you know this relationship isn't serious and he is still free to do what he wants. It's his way of letting you know that you aren't a deciding factor in where he goes and what he does. Men typically communicate through actions more than words, so his behavior is telling you exactly where he stands.

3. He Tells You He Doesn't Want A Relationship

This seems like an obvious one, but unfortunately, it's not! In fact, I think the most common relationship in this day and age is the *non-relationship*, or the *situationship,* when you're dating a guy and you're basically boyfriend/girlfriend aside from the fact that you're not.

The simple truth is this: when a guy says he doesn't want a relationship, what he's really saying is he doesn't want a relationship with *you*.

I know you think you're the exception and your situation is different. I've been there and I'm telling you, you're not and it isn't. You're like every other girl in a non-relationship. You're a great girl who maybe sold herself a little short and is in a situation where the guy calls all the shots and is just taking you along for the ride as you sit patiently in the back seat, waiting for him to decide if you're "good enough."

If he tells you he doesn't want to be in a relationship, or he has "commitment issues," or hates labels, just take it at face value, do yourself a favor, and move on. Trust me, if he *really* likes you he won't let you go so easily. And if he does let you go...he just was never invested enough in the first place, and that's not a loss.

4. He Doesn't Take You On Real Dates

If your dates consist of you going over to his place and watching a movie or you cooking for him, then he isn't taking you or the relationship very seriously.

When a guy is invested in you and cares about you, he wants to go out of his way to impress you and show you he cares. I know most women don't feel this way but trust me, when a guy likes you, it's *obvious.*

If he puts in the bare minimum when it comes to dates it means he doesn't feel like you're worth the effort. Are there exceptions? Sometimes. But even if a guy is jobless and broke and doesn't have the money to take you out, he'll find some sort of cheap and creative way to show you he cares.

When a guy cares about a woman and sees a future with her, he wants to bring her into his world as much as possible. He wants to introduce her to the things he likes: movies, music, books, hobbies. These aren't things that require much of a financial investment but they speak volumes about his level of *emotional investment.*

If you're the only one making the effort to keep the spark alive and do special things, it's a sign that he isn't very invested in you.

5. He Won't Introduce You To His Family

A lot of women make the mistake of thinking that meeting a guy's friends is a big deal. Maybe some guys view this as a big deal, but most don't. Maybe he just wants to show you off because you're hot, or maybe he just doesn't think much of introducing girls to his friends. I have plenty of friends and clients who looked at meeting his friends as the Holy Grail...the telltale sign that he's all in, he's committed. It's not. Meeting his family is where it's at. (Side note: while meeting his friends isn't the biggest deal, if he won't introduce you to them it's a definite red flag.)

When you're in a relationship, talk of meeting the family should come up. Maybe you don't meet them right away, but he should give you some sort of indication that it's on the horizon. At the very least, he should let you know that his family is aware of your existence.

If he doesn't talk about his family, or changes the subject anytime you bring them up, it's a sign that he has no intention of making the introduction.

As I mentioned earlier, when a man is serious about a woman, he brings her into his world. By keeping you away from his family, he's essentially saying he doesn't see you being in his world for the long run.

I should point out that there are guys who introduce almost every girl they date to their families and don't really see it as a big deal...and maybe their families are used to this revolving door of girlfriends. However, if he's serious about you, he will take this meeting a little more seriously than he has in the past. He'll be excited, and maybe a little nervous about you meeting them because he really wants them to like you, and for you to like them. If he doesn't really seem to care, then even if he does introduce you to them it's a sign he isn't fully invested in having a future with you.

The Pseudo-Relationship (Or "Situationship")

A pseudo-relationship can take on many forms, but in essence it's a relationship with some mutual interest and attraction but no real commitment. The lack of commitment is usually because one person is a little less interested and invested than the other. I can't even count how many of these types of relationships I've been in. If the definition of insanity really is doing the same thing over and over but expecting different results then I should have been locked away in a padded room many times over! I kept winding up in situations where I was kind of in a relationship but not really, always hoping it would turn into one, but it never did. It rarely does.

Here is how it usually goes. Girl meets boy, sparks ignite, they enter the "talking phase," then they start hanging out...everything seems to be going well. He seems really into her, so much so that her guard comes down, she *really* starts to like him, she starts envisioning all the possibilities, she gets her hopes up...but then it all comes crashing down when he tells her he likes things the way they are, he doesn't like labels, he isn't ready for a commitment.

Now she's a little stuck. His reasons are valid...he *does* have a lot going on in his life, so it makes sense he isn't ready to commit, right? And things *are* great as is, why rock the boat? She gives him space and she's always there, just waiting in the wings. He gets to have his freedom, but it's at the expense of her need for stability.

She is stuck in a position of waiting to be chosen. She wants him, he knows that. And he likes her, but he is still leaving the door open for other possibilities and this hurts. How can it not?

She continues to invest in him, hoping that all her work will pay off and he will reciprocate, but the opposite happens. He begins to take her for granted and she feels more and more desperate to win his love and affection.

So why does this happen?

Well, it could be the wrong time. And the right person at the wrong time is the wrong person. If he's not ready to commit, that's fine. But it's not your problem and you should never put yourself in a situation of waiting around for him to be ready and to choose you.

Next, it's possible that while he does like you...he just doesn't like you enough...

When A Guy Likes You...But Not Enough

One of the biggest problems in the world of dating and relationships is when a guy likes you, but not enough.

The fact is, when a guy likes you, it's clear. As in, clear as day, no room for error, no signs to interpret or messages to uncover. So then why is the most asked question: *Does he like me?*

It's a miserable feeling to invest your time and emotions into someone when you're not sure where he stands. Through time, experience, and research, I've learned that when you have to question how he feels...you already have your answer. He likes you, just not enough.

The problem is that so many of us get caught in a trap of trying to figure out why. We can't understand how he can say so many sweet things, how he can be so open and present when he's with us, how everything can feel so right when we're with him...yet he can't give us what we really want, which is usually a committed relationship.

Maybe he has valid reasons. Maybe he *is* under a lot of pressure at work, maybe his parents' divorce when he was a kid really *did* make him stop believing in monogamy, maybe the ex-girlfriend who cheated on him really *did* destroy his ability to trust, maybe he *is* terrified of commitment...the reasons don't matter, the facts do. And if a guy says he doesn't want to be in a relationship with you, he means it.

He probably does care about you, he does enjoy spending time with you, he does like you...he just doesn't like you enough. Maybe it's because he's incapable of liking someone past a certain point (a point that would lead to a relationship), or maybe he just doesn't see himself with someone like you for reasons beyond your control. It doesn't matter.

If he likes spending time with you and hanging out, but doesn't want to be official...he likes you, he just doesn't like you enough.

If you run into each other here and there and talk for hours and maybe even hook up, but you don't hear from him after...he likes you, he just doesn't like you enough.

If you've been seeing each other for a while and he refuses to be exclusive, or doesn't want to put a label on it...he likes you, he just doesn't like you enough.

If he isn't giving you the commitment you want...he likes you, he just doesn't like you enough.

Sadly, most women believe a man not liking them enough is a reflection on them, and they make it their problem. They think if only they did more for him, if only they were prettier, if only they could help him learn to trust again, if only they hadn't said this and instead had said that...everything would be different. It wouldn't. If this is how he feels, nothing you say or do will change that. His issues are his issues. You pave the way for a lot of unnecessary hurt when you make them yours.

Remember what I said earlier about two things being true at the same time? Well it applies here as well. He can like you and think you're amazing and hot and awesome and all the things...but just not want to be with you. Why doesn't he want to be with you? Because not everyone is a match and that's fine!

When a guy shows a genuine interest in who you are and what you like, he is invested. And when he takes the information gathered about what you like and goes out of his way to give it to you, he is in love.

So stop torturing yourself with guessing games that will give you as much information as plucking petals off a rose. And stop waiting to hear the words.

Instead, look at the *actions*. Look at what he does, how he treats you, how he tries to make you happy. He may not always get it right, but that's not what matters. What matters is the intention.

When it comes to love, the rule to live by is never allow yourself to care for someone who hasn't shown he cares about making you happy. This is why it's best to keep relationships slow and steady in the beginning, it'll give you a better sense of the man you're dealing with.

The Placeholder

It's time to get blunt and bring on a dose of honest truth. A placeholder relationship usually occurs when a guy isn't into a girl enough to commit...but is into her enough to keep her around for companionship, emotional support, and sex.

It's not your typical "friends-with-benefits" situation because it's more than just sex. There is a real emotional connection in addition to the physical one.

The feelings are real which is why the woman has such a hard time walking away. There is so much potential there, *if only* he could step up and give the relationship a real chance. But he just doesn't and there could be a variety of reasons.

It's possible he thinks he can do better, maybe she has some deal-breaker qualities that are fine for now but wouldn't work long term, or maybe something just doesn't feel right. I've interviewed countless men over the years and I can't even tell you how many times I've heard "It was just a feeling..." when asked why they didn't commit to certain women, even ones they really liked.

So he knows he doesn't really see a future, but he keeps her around. Now you may be tempted to label him a narcissist, and some guys are so we can classify that as a maybe, but he also keeps her around because she seems to *want* to be there. She is staying even though he's been pretty clear about his feelings and intentions.

And here is the kicker: you can't really blame him for that because your time is *your* responsibility. I know you may be tempted to lash out at him over "taking advantage" of you, but you stayed because you wanted to. You stayed because you were getting something out of the situation. So don't waste your energy being mad, use it to be even *better* for your next relationship.

A placeholder relationship like this can drag on for months or even years. Eventually, maybe the guy does find what he's been looking for and he'll drop his current girl like a hot potato. He may feel bad about it, but at the same time he rationalizes that it was never a "real" relationship, so this was always how it was going to play out.

It's possible the guy never had any intention of settling down or committing...that's why you believed him when he said now wasn't the right time. But then something shifted in his life, or maybe he met the right person.

The placeholder relationship can make things really comfortable for the guy. He can do whatever he wants and she'll always be there. If he's in a low place in his life, she's his emotional support; his crutch. And while that's comforting, it doesn't feel good to a man, it makes him feel like a pathetic loser.

So when someone else comes along and he pursues that...it's not necessarily because she's better than you, he just sees it as an opportunity to start anew and be with a woman who doesn't see him as a loser.

You feel used and betrayed. You think he owes you something because of everything you've done for him. I know. I've lived it too. But don't let it make you jaded or bitter, because that won't serve you. Instead, use these feelings to set a solid boundary. One that states, "I will never commit myself to someone who is not committed to me."

The Friend Who Seems Like Something More

I get a lot of questions about the "friend zone," usually from women who are trying to break out of it and into the relationship zone.

Of all the relationship issues out there, I think this is the easiest one to address.

First, I will say I relate to the confusion. Many years ago I met a guy I thought would be perfect for me, and I was crushed when I found out he had told a friend of mine (who had suggested he ask me out) that he didn't want to date me because he was good friends with some of my good friends, including my roommate, and didn't want things to get "weird."

I naively took his excuse as fact and was determined to show him that I was a cool girl and if he dated me, there would be zero weirdness. I made a point of letting him know that I run a website with my ex-boyfriend (talk about overcoming a weird situation!) and have stayed friends with a lot of guys I've dated in the past. I took every opportunity that presented itself to let him know that dating me carries zero weirdness. I also went on a pathetic quest to prove to him how great we would be together and to highlight how much we had in common. (I shudder thinking back on this now!)

The point is, I made a mistake that a lot of women make when a guy uses the old "I don't want to ruin the friendship" excuse. We take that as fact and believe if it weren't for that he would ask us out and we'd live happily ever after.

One night I brought a friend to another friend's birthday party where my crush also happened to be. The second he saw her he had that look. I didn't want to admit what was happening, but it was clear. He was into her. They flirted all night, exchanged numbers, and they started dating. And he did not have one ounce of fear of ruining any friendship with me or any of our other mutual friends.

I'm not saying you can't ever get out of the friend zone with a guy, because it is possible in some cases, but I am saying it's a waste of time to put all your energy into trying. It's a waste of time to tally up the "signs" to try to figure out if he likes you as more than a friend because no guy is ever genuinely concerned with ruining the friendship! If a guy really likes a girl, the last thought that will cross his mind is fear of ruining the friendship. I have posed this question to countless men and the answer is always the same: no man is ever worried about ruining the friendship with a girl he likes.

If a guy says he doesn't want to date you because he doesn't want to ruin the friendship or make things weird with your mutual friends, he's probably just trying to spare your feelings; the real reasons is most likely that while he enjoys hanging out with you, he doesn't feel enough of a romantic attraction to want to take things further. This doesn't change even if you and he have hooked up. A hook up (or multiple hook ups) just means he is somewhat attracted to you, but again, not enough to want to date you. Because if he wanted to, he would.

Now there is maybe only one other reason why a guy you're friends with might like you but not ask you out, and that's if he's afraid of being rejected.

Most men are terrified of rejection and will do anything to avoid it. Getting around this one is easy enough, though—just indicate that you're interested in him. You don't need to be obvious about it, just give him something to go on, anything that lets him know he won't be rejected if he asks you out. If he knows you're interested and won't reject him and he has feelings for you, he will pursue you. There won't be any talk of ruining the friendship. It goes against a man's nature to see an opportunity to get something he wants and not take it.

What if you show him you're interested and he reciprocates, but then tells you he can't be in a relationship right now? Well then, forget it. If what you want is a relationship, don't spend time on someone who can't or won't give you that. In these cases nothing you do will talk him out of it so it's best to just stay friends and continue exploring your options.

OK, now let's review:

> No man is ever afraid of ruining the friendship.

> Plotting ways to get out of the friend zone is a waste of time and will leave you with nothing but shameful memories.

> The primary reason a guy might like you and not ask you out is that he's afraid of being rejected. All you need to do is demonstrate a small amount of interest so he knows he won't be rejected and humiliated if he asks you out.

Why We Stay In Bad Relationships

I know all too well how hard it is to extricate yourself from a bad relationship. You've invested so much time and energy into the situation and refuse to accept things as they really are.

You pay attention to the things you want to hear and disregard all the red flags because you want this relationship to mean something, and you just can't accept that he doesn't reciprocate your feelings. You cling to the belief that things would be different if only XYZ were no longer an issue.

When things are good, they are so good. When they're bad, you cling to the good memories, rationalizing reasons to stay. And you do. You stay until *he* goes and you're left crushed, and then the pain comes flooding in.

You may think the reason it hurts so much is because he was the perfect guy for you and you let him get away. But that's not it. I think the reason it hurts so much when these situations end is because you're left trying to understand how it is that a smart, intuitive woman such as yourself could ignore so many blatant red flags and stay with a guy who didn't treat her right. You feel like you've sold yourself short, like you've compromised your values and gone against what you know to be true, and it's a miserable feeling.

You feel like he took something from you and now there's a void you need to fill. And he did, and you do.

He took advantage of you, he allowed you to keep investing even though he was never on the same page. He made it seem safe for you to be vulnerable with him, and you felt understood and connected. Vulnerability is a gift, and when someone exploits that gift, it can be unbearable.

Imagine you're in the middle of Times Square and a weird, crazy-looking guy comes up to you and asks for directions. You're a nice person so you oblige, but then later notice that your wallet is missing. You are not surprised in the least—you kind of knew that would happen. Oh well, time to cancel the credit cards and order a new driver's license.

Now let's say a handsome, charming, British man approaches you in Times Square asking for directions. You're taken by his sexy accent and dreamy eyes. You chat for a while and give him the 411 on NYC and all the places to visit. He leaves and you reach for your wallet...and it's gone. You're floored. Your thought process will probably be something like this: *How could I have been so stupid? I can't believe I fell for that! There must be something wrong with me...am I really that naive? I thought he was interested in me, what a fool I am! Or maybe he was just hitting on me. Maybe I dropped my wallet...*

I don't think I need to spell out the difference between these two scenarios; it's pretty clear.

When we feel like we've compromised our values and better judgment, it hurts. We don't want to believe we could have been so foolish, so we try to find another reason, another explanation, one that makes us less culpable.

So why do we do it? Why do we stay in relationships when we aren't being respected, when our emotional needs get dismissed, when we feel bad about ourselves, when we're insulted, when we're treated like crap? We would never tolerate such things from a job or a friendship—we would leave. But in romantic relationships we stay.

Here are some of the core reasons:

1. You Don't Want To Believe You Could Stay With Someone Who Treats You Badly

So you convince yourself that's not what's happening. I remember when I was in my really bad relationship a friend approached me and expressed her concerns. She said she didn't think he was treating me right and I should get out of the relationship. This was still early on and had I listened, I would have saved myself a significant amount of pain.

But I didn't listen. Instead I got extremely defensive and told her, and this is a direct quote, "You don't know what you're talking about—he treats me like gold!" And I really believed it. I had convinced myself that the kind things he did amounted to gold, and everything else he did could just be ignored because gold shines brighter than that stuff, anyway!

I really cared about him and didn't want to believe that someone I cared about could treat me badly, so I created a different story. In my story nothing was *that* bad; I was probably just exaggerating his bad behavior. He probably didn't mean those nasty things he said. He was stressed out and sad and couldn't always control his temper so none of that bad stuff counted, what counted was the good stuff!

The human mind has an extraordinary ability to write its own version of reality, and that's what mine did. It just seemed easier than accepting that maybe, possibly, I was in a bad relationship.

2. You Don't Believe You Deserve Better

You may not actively believe you don't deserve better, but somewhere deep down that's how you feel. Don't dismiss the power of the subconscious mind; it is the puppet master behind almost everything we do. If you've developed a belief at some point that you are unworthy of love, then you won't attract healthy, happy love. You'll stay in bad relationships because that's what you think you deserve and what you believe to be normal. And if all you've had are bad relationships, you won't really have a basis for comparison. Since all you know is being treated like crap, then crap is what you'll come to expect.

Eventually you might figure it's better to stay in this type of relationship than have no relationship at all. You might start having a fatalistic belief that this is the kind of relationship that was just designated for you.

Obviously this is a very dangerous belief that can lead to a lot of unhealthy choices. While it would be nice to just flip a mental switch and instantly wire yourself to believe that you're worthy of love, changing deeply held beliefs about yourself takes a bit more work. But it is possible! Some can do it on their own, but working with a great therapist can really expedite the process.

3. You Have Excessive Empathy

Excessive empathy is a term I came up with to explain the mostly female propensity to make excuses for a guy based on his potential rather than his current behavior. A woman's empathy kicks into gear when she sees a guy acting badly, but also thinks she sees the good guy he *could* be if only he got over his issues.

You make excuses for him: he had a rough childhood, he went through a bad breakup, he's depressed, he hates his job, he's in debt...whatever it is, you see that thing as the cause of his bad behavior and believe because of that it's not his fault. You figure that as soon as he overcomes that one thing, everything will be different.

Now I'm not saying you shouldn't ever give anyone the benefit of the doubt, but you need to hold people accountable for their bad behavior, even while being compassionate about the root cause for it. You also need to realize that you can't change another person, you can't get over his issues for him, you can't solve his problems, and you can't fix his life. You can inspire change and you can be there for support, but you can't do it for him. A person can only help himself. When you become his fixer, then you risk forming an unhealthy, codependent relationship.

If he isn't actively working on himself and trying to be a better man, then there is nothing you can do. Compassion is a wonderful virtue, but it needs limits, otherwise you run a real risk of having your heart broken.

If you're in a relationship where you feel bad about yourself, where you aren't being treated with respect, where you find yourself constantly making excuses for him, where other people in your life are expressing concern, where you don't even feel like yourself anymore, then it's time to take some space and do some real thinking about whether this relationship is something you need in your life.

If you have dated guys who treat you like crap in the past, or if you are currently involved with a guy you know doesn't treat you the way you deserve, ask yourself the following questions:

> What thoughts/behaviors/beliefs led you into this relationship?

> What did you bring to the relationship that was good and that you would want to use in your next relationship?

> What did you do in this relationship that you never want to do again?

> Why did you stay in this relationship even though it didn't feel good? What were you getting out of it?

> What need did he fulfill for you?

> I'll get into this concept more in the next chapter on what ruins relationships, so keep reading!

Remember this: People aren't that complicated. If someone says they don't want to be in a relationship, they mean it. If they aren't taking steps to be with you, it's because they don't want to. If you can't tell how they feel, then you actually already know how they feel.

CHAPTER 5

How to Stop Self-Sabotaging & Ruining Your Relationships

"To acquire love...fill yourself up with it until you become a magnet." —*Charles F. Haanel*

Sometimes we are our own worst enemies and sabotage our chances of getting what we really want. Relationship, career, fitness...we can derail ourselves in all areas of life. It's a hard pill to swallow...when there's no one to blame.

I've been writing about relationships for years and can't help but notice patterns in where women go wrong. It's not anyone's fault. No one sets out with bad intentions, trying to sabotage their relationship. Usually, all a woman wants is to keep her relationship strong and happy. She wants it to last, but oftentimes she still ends up doing things that can push a guy away and ruin a relationship.

One area where people go wrong is in not working on themselves and letting less than ideal character traits go unchecked. I think that on the one hand we'd like to believe that this is the way we are and the person we're with should just take it or leave it, on the other hand we realize that isn't really the healthiest attitude, especially when it comes to negative tendencies like being insecure, clingy, needy, jealous, vengeful, hostile and on and on.

Yeah, being this way might be "yourself," but it's the worst of you. Why not make an effort to refine those weak spots and be your best self? This is how you win.

A lot of women just don't fully understand how men operate, or how a woman's behavior impacts the relationship dynamic overall. Now I know you may want to reflexively get mad at me and say I'm blaming women, but I'm not. I could sugarcoat things for you and say you're right and men are always wrong, but I wouldn't be helping you or doing you any favors.

Look, all we can do in life is focus on that which is under our control. And you only have control over yourself. You can't control how other people feel about you. All you can do is bring your best to the table and trust that things will work out as they are meant to.

Why The Guys You Want Don't Want You

One of the most frustrating and puzzling relationship issues is determining why the guys you want don't seem to want you.

Here is how it usually goes. You get involved with a guy that you really like who just doesn't seem to be as interested. He's into it, he's attracted, he likes hanging out with you, but he's not quite there. You, on the other hand, have gone all in and the fact that he isn't at the same point leaves you with a constant feeling of unease just beneath the surface.

If you have been in several situations like this, you might start to wonder if it's you, if you're doing something wrong. But then how can that be when all these other guys, the ones you don't want, are desperate to date you? Why is it that the commitment and the proclamations of love and devotion only seem to come from the guys you don't want and not the ones you do?

Well, these are the most likely reasons why.

1. You Want Him

One of the biggest reasons the guys you want don't want you comes down to the simple fact that you *want* them. Or rather, want them a little too much and for reasons that are not what you think.

When we want something, it represents something to us and we internalize the having of that thing as meaning something about us. If we can get the guy, then we're validated, we're worthy of love, we have succeeded. If we can't get him to want us, then there is something wrong with us; we are flawed and unlovable.

It's not just a relationship thing. We do this with money, with jobs, with status, with Instagram likes. Measuring your worth on external factors is a recipe for feeling chronically unfulfilled.

Wanting puts you into agenda mode. You meet a guy who has a set of qualities that you want in a man and you make it your mission to have him. From that point on you measure your interactions with him in terms of whether they're getting you closer to, or further from, your ultimate goal. When you have an agenda, you are interacting with the thoughts in your mind and this prevents you from building a genuine connection, because how can you connect when you're not really there?

2. You Stress Over How He Feels

When you want a guy and aren't sure if he wants you back, your mind can't help but stress over how he feels. You tally up the signs he likes you go over every interaction, you read into every single text looking for clues. This obsessive line of thinking transmits a desperate, needy vibe that people can intuitively pick up on.

When you go on a quest to figure out how he feels, your fears and insecurities will inevitably get activated and this will come across and a guy (and people in general) can always pick up on an energy or a vibe.

It doesn't matter what you do, it's the *intention* behind it.

If you are acting a certain way in order to make him feel a certain way about you, he will intuitively sense that you aren't genuine, that you are trying to get something from him, and his guard will instinctively go up because that's how all people naturally respond when we sense someone has ulterior motives.

It's much like a car salesman who comes up to you and is all nice and jovial and seemingly interested in you as a person. You don't buy it because you know that, while he might be very nice and might like you very much, he is really just trying to sell you something and that is driving all his behaviors.

3. Too Much Pressure

It doesn't matter if you come out and ask him where things are going or if he has feelings for you, if you mentally want something from a guy (in this case, a commitment), he will know and will feel pressured.

Even if you're just waiting by the phone for his text, he will feel it. It's just an energy that gets sent out, and believe me I'm not a super New-Age person, but it's true. We can usually sense when someone wants something from us. This is why the guys you aren't so into are usually so into you; because there's no pressure. You're just feeling it out and testing the waters and he feels a sense of freedom in the relationship. He essentially has the freedom to *choose you*, whereas with the guys you really want, you are on a quest to be *chosen*.

Here is a very important thing to realize about how men fall in love. Men usually fall for a woman based on how they feel when they're around her.

Women, on the other hand, usually have a mental checklist. If a guy checks off enough boxes, she'll see him as a potential romantic partner and will begin to invest and get excited about the possibilities.

Sure, most men have a certain "type," but they rarely go out seeking a specific set of qualities. What makes a man commit is how he feels in your presence. When he feels pressured in any way, then it leaves little room for him to feel anything else and it causes him to lose whatever interest he had in you.

4. You Aren't Connecting With Him In A Meaningful Way

As I said, when you have an agenda, you are engaging with the thoughts in your head, and not with the person in front of you. A lot of times, we convince ourselves that we like a guy just because he matches up with our dating checklist, not because we have gotten to know who he truly is at his core.

No man wants to feel like he's filling a slot that any other dude could easily occupy. Maybe you like that he's good-looking, employed, funny, tall, nice, etc., but there are millions of other guys like that out there.

A guy wants to feel chosen because of how great *he* is, because of who he is at his core, not because he meets some minimum requirement of characteristics. (And women feel the same way!)

A lot of the time, the guys you want don't want you because you don't make an effort to truly connect with him as a person. You see him as a means to an end, an opportunity to have a boyfriend and settle down, a chance to feel good about yourself and worthy, without really taking the time to get to know him.

When you connect with a man, he feels safe. And as I explained, a man bonds with a woman when he feels good in her presence and feeling safe always feels good.

5. You Choose The Guys Who Can't Give You What You Want

Lastly, a reason why the guys you want don't want you is that you're going after guys who aren't in a position to be capable of having any sort of relationship.

These are the guys who are selfish or in a bad place or confused about what they want or are nowhere near ready for a relationship. I can relate to this one the most because it was my pattern for far too long.

Going for guys like this can be a form of self-sabotage. It can happen when deep down you feel unworthy, you feel not good enough. And these feelings are usually rooted in childhood pain and trauma.

So deep down you have these beliefs about yourself, and then you go out into the world and try to date and try to find a partner but you only seem drawn to the ones who don't want you. And this is because the subconscious mind is always looking to prove itself right. If you believe you are unworthy, you will be drawn to partners who make you feel that way.

When a guy does show genuine interest, you may be put off because this doesn't align with how you see yourself. You don't truly like yourself and you, again this is subconscious, believe anyone who does like or love you must be fatally flawed.

If you were nodding along with this last section in pained recognition, I feel you on a deep level. Because this was me. And I won't say it was an easy road, but with the right therapist, the right self-help books, and the motivation to really change, I was able to overcome this. My relationships up until that point were always lopsided. Either it was me obsessed with a guy who wasn't feeling it, or a guy hopelessly in love with me and me trying to scrape up any romantic feelings I could find in my hollow heart.

It was a hopeless pattern and until I really faced the darkness within me and made the resolute decision to heal, I thought I would spend my life stuck in that sad loop of chasing emotionally unavailable and damaged me. But I didn't. Once I broke free I saw my behavior for what it was and those types of guys lost all appeal to me. I realized I was valuable and worthy and I had no time for anyone who didn't see it too.

I knew I had truly healed when I started dating my husband and the fact that he really liked me didn't turn me off at all, it actually made me like him even more.

We will talk more about healing and being your best self in Chapter 6 and I'll give you a lot of tips and tools, but first let's talk more about how you may be screwing things up.

How To Ruin A Budding Relationship

The beginning of a relationship is often the most confusing time, a time when everything seems precarious and you don't quite know where you stand or where, if anywhere, the relationship is going.

Men and women are different and so the way they experience and process relationships is different. Men tend to be much more in the moment. If the relationship is enjoyable in the here and now, they're happy. If it's unpleasant, they either distance themselves or leave. Women, on the other hand, tend to get stuck in where the relationship is going and the "clues," both real and imagined, that will supposedly give them the answer. In the midst of this quest to figure out what's going on and where a man stands, women often lose sight of what's important (the actual relationship, and how it is in the here and now).

Here are five things you might unknowingly be doing that can ruin your relationship:

1. Jumping The Gun

This scenario might sound familiar to you. You meet a guy and instantly hit it off. You go out a few times and realize that he basically has every quality you want in a man. You don't want to do it, but you can't help but think how perfect it would be if it worked out and you ended up together. You think about all the crazy coincidences that led to your meeting him (if there weren't any, you'll find some to make this a great "how we met" story!) and feel certain that this union was written in the stars. You're not even official with him yet, but you could never conceive of dating another guy —that would almost be like having an affair! You're sure this guy is the one, you're positive of it. You have an amazing time together, you talk for hours, things are great, except you're on two completely different pages!

What's the harm, you might wonder, it's not like he *knows* you've already picked out the china pattern for your wedding registry. Oh, but he does. They always do.

Men are very much in tune with the vibe and energy a woman gives off. And when a man feels that pressure, even the slightest pressure, he will back off. When this happens, you will of course start to panic and may cling even tighter, thinking you'd be a fool to let the love of your life slip away! The more you push, the more he pulls away, until there's nothing left but the memory of him and the pain of thinking what might have been.

Due to the nature of my career, people talk to me about their relationships. *A lot.* I hear it from guys and I hear it from girls. The funny thing I've noticed is that when a girlfriend starts dating a new guy and I ask her how it's going, she'll usually say something like "It's great! I can totally see myself marrying someone like him." When I talk to my guy friends about a new girl, they'll usually say, "She's great, I definitely want to go out with her again." So the woman is planning the wedding while the guy is planning the next date. Talk about worlds apart.

You have to just relax and be in the moment and stop thinking of what the future might hold and solving problems that don't even exist yet. On a date, the only thing you should be thinking about is if you want to go on another date.

The important thing to realize about most men is that they're very in the moment. Women can be, too, but more often they can't help but get a little overzealous when a promising prospect comes along. Like I said, this sort of pressure can be a huge turn-off and can transform a promising relationship into a nonexistent one real fast. So take a breath, quiet the chatter in your mind, and focus on enjoying your relationship for what it is, as it is, right here and right now.

2. Overanalyzing

Overanalyzing ties into the jumping too many steps ahead because they're both essentially rooted in fear.

You meet a great guy and you can't help but feel a little worried that your feelings won't be reciprocated. In an attempt to protect yourself, you look at the "clues" in his behavior and try to figure out what everything means. If something seems like a bad sign, you focus on solving it. You pick apart his texts and emails, you debate endlessly over what to respond and whether an emoticon would seem cheesy or cute, you spend hours talking to your friends about why he's taking so long to text back and what it means and what he might be up to. You replay every moment of every interaction with him, keeping a tally of the signs he likes you and signs he doesn't. It's exhausting.

The truth is, 90% of relationship problems wouldn't exist if women would stop obsessing and analyzing and just go with it. It's the *overthinking* that causes problems to emerge out of nowhere. And this is true of all areas of your life, not just relationships. When has overthinking ever led you to a good place?

What's more, the more time you spend thinking and talking about him, the more you're investing in him and the more hurt you'll be if the relationship ends. Guys like their relationships and their lives to be simple and drama free. The most attractive woman to a guy is one who goes with the flow and can be present in the relationship without putting too much pressure on it. If you're consumed with your anxious, frenzied thoughts, you'll be too busy worrying about the relationship to actually enjoy being in it.

The best attitude to have is one where you feel happy with your guy, but would be OK without him. How do you do this? Just tell yourself, as many times as you need to, "I will be OK no matter what. I was OK before him and I will be OK after him."

Don't waste your time trying to figure out if he likes you and what he meant when he said XYZ, instead be confident and trust that he does like you. Believing others like you increases the chances that they will. It makes sense when you think about it. If you believe someone likes you, you'll be relaxed and at ease around them. You'll be warm and inviting and more open around them. Acting this way increases the chances that they will come to like you.

And if for whatever reason he doesn't, who cares?! All that means is he isn't the right guy for you because the right guy for you *wants* to be with you. Be grateful that he had the clarity to realize you aren't a match because he freed you up to meet the guy who *is* right for you.

3. Acting Official Before You're Actually Official

OK now, this is by far the biggest relationship-ruining mistake. Girl meets boy, girl really, *really* likes boy, girl cuts off all other potential suitors and focuses exclusively on boy even though they never decided to be exclusive. How this usually turns out is boy ends up telling girl "I like our relationship as it is and don't want to label it," and girl is devastated but stays in the relationship anyway, hoping he'll change his mind.

Look, I know it's tough to keep your options open when you find someone who shines so much brighter than the rest, but you cannot act like his partner until you are his partner. Why? Because most people are not going to willingly deepen a level of commitment unless they have to.

If you don't necessarily want to date multiple people at a time, that's fine, just keep yourself mentally open to the possibilities. Don't take down your online dating profiles or prioritize them over everything else in your life until he reciprocates.

Remember, you don't get a man to invest in you by investing in him, you get it by leaving the space for him to choose you and invest in you. The choice for him is gone when you commit yourself fully before a discussion has even been had.

4. Dropping Your Life For Him

This is another common relationship trap. You start seeing a guy, you spend more and more time together, and suddenly he is just about the only thing you have going on in your life. You ditch your friends for him, don't go to the gym as often, don't go to book club. The reason this guy was drawn to you in the first place was because you had a well-rounded, fulfilling life that you enjoyed. You can't expect to abandon the things that make you who you are and have him feel the same level of attraction and intrigue towards you.

When you abandon all the things that make you *you*, not only does it make you less attractive to him, it also creates an unspoken expectation that he is going to fill in the empty space and be the sole source of your happiness and fulfillment. That is way too much pressure for anyone!

Also, if you give up your life for him and come to expect him to do the same for you, he will begin to resent you for taking away his freedom.

The point is, don't stop being who you were before the relationship after you're in it. Keep your life balanced, fun, and fulfilling, with many sources of happiness.

5. Not Seeing The Relationship For What It Is

When it comes to relationships, the devil is in the delusions. A lot of us have a truly amazing ability to see exactly what we want to see and ignore the truth in front of us.

A guy might say he doesn't want a relationship with you, but you stick around, knowing with certainty that he'll change his mind. You convince yourself that he doesn't really mean it. You are positive that he cares about you because he took you to a fancy restaurant, he said he missed you, he told you about his hopes and dreams. Any nice thing he said or did from the time you met is tallied up and used as proof that he really cares. And all the stuff he did that indicates he isn't serious? Well, we can just ignore those and take a glass-half-full sort of approach!

Before entering into a relationship, you must be clear with yourself about exactly what you want. If you're not, then it's far too easy to get caught up in something you don't want. I get so many questions from women who are upset or angry at their guy for reasons that are completely invalid. For instance, he told her he doesn't want to be exclusive, she continues seeing him anyway, and then she gets mad at him when she catches him texting another girl. So she's mad at him for not acting like he's in a real relationship even though they are not in a real relationship.

Know the kind of relationship you want and know that you deserve to have it and you don't need to settle for some half-baked version of it. It's OK to admit that you want to get married or to be in a committed relationship. I know in this day and age it's considered passé for women to admit to such things—instead we're supposed to be independent and strong and not need a man—but if that's what you want, give yourself permission to want it. The first step to getting what you want is knowing what it is.

6. Not Seeing The Guy For Who He Is

When it comes to relationships, most women have a tendency to focus on the potential of the guy they're dating more than on who he actually is at that point in time. Helping a man reach his full potential can be an incredible and beautiful thing. However, it can take a toll on you if you let this desire run wild, and that is where things get sticky.

For instance, a woman in an abusive relationship may find herself unable to leave because although she knows this isn't the kind of relationship she wants and this isn't the way she deserves to be treated, she sees the good guy the abuser could be and doesn't want to let him go, even though the person in her head doesn't even really exist.

That's the problem with toxic relationships, they're not toxic *all* the time. There also can be a lot of good mixed in the toxicity and a lot of us can't help but try to take those seeds of goodness and turn them into. Beautiful garden.

I think we've all found ourselves in these kinds of situations, whether it be physical abuse, emotional abuse, codependence, a toxic relationship, or just a bad relationship.

A friend of mine started dating the man of her dreams a few years ago. He literally checked every box on her long list of ideal man traits. At first, everything was amazing. He was sweet, attentive, and romantic. It was going so well she felt like she was starring in her very own romantic comedy! But then things started to change.

As things got more serious, his darker side came out. He gradually became very critical of her and his derogatory remarks and snide comments became more and more frequent. He was also struggling with his own issues; he felt depressed, he didn't like his job and wanted to change fields, and he felt dissatisfied with his life overall. She tried to help, but it only made things worse, and he started blaming her for the way he was feeling. Any time she tried to talk about it he would withdraw and go cold and shut her out completely.

Even though she felt completely alone in the relationship and no longer confident in herself due to his biting insults, she stayed as committed as ever. Not only that, she saw it all as her fault. She knew he had the ability to be great; he had been great earlier in their relationship so maybe it was her fault he'd changed.

She became completely blind to the man he actually was and focused exclusively on the man he could be. The more he retreated, the more she desperately tried to win him back—to motivate him, to inspire him, to turn him into the man she thought he was deep down. Unfortunately, her efforts were in vain. Not only didn't he change, he eventually dumped her and didn't look back. She was left crushed and broken-hearted, and it took her years to pick up the pieces. He, on the other hand, moved on without missing a beat and quickly got engaged and married to someone else. Part of the reason she had a harder time moving on was because of how much she'd invested in and given to the relationship. And the reason she'd invested so heavily was partly because of her love for him, but mostly because of her love for who she thought he was deep down and could become.

Being able to see someone else's potential is a very powerful skill that we women are blessed with. However, it has to be kept in its place. Believing in someone and helping him through difficulties is one thing. Staying in a relationship with a man who is incapable of giving you what you need and who ends up dragging you down is quite another.

This situation will make him feel like a failure for not being what you want, and it will make you feel like a failure for not succeeding in getting him to be the man you know he's capable of being.

In a relationship, you have to accept the person for who they are, exactly as they are, and you have to assume they aren't going to change.

If it's a healthy relationship where both parties are in stable places emotionally, you will naturally bring out the best in one another, including each other's hidden potential. If it's an unhealthy relationship, you will only tear each other down.

Having a bad day or a bad week is understandable, but that's not what I'm talking about. What I'm talking about is a continued pattern of unacceptable behavior.

7. You're Emotionally Unavailable

Plot twist! The problem isn't only women being too needy or desperate. You can have the same relationship problems by being too unavailable.

I often get messages like this: *Sabrina, you talk a lot about women being too needy and that's why they can't get a guy but I'm not like that at all. I'm independent and never act needy in relationships but guys never seem to want to go on more than a few dates with me.*

When I work with these types of women I see a common theme: They are very guarded and closed off. A lot of them haven't healed from having their hearts broken in the past and they have walls up.

The guys who date these kinds of women often say they lost interest because something was missing, they can't even put their finger on what it was—they found her attractive, cool, interesting, etc. but there was just a missing piece. Usually, it's her emotional detachment that's the missing piece. You can't really form a connection with someone who isn't truly there.

Another reason for this is that emotionally unavailable women sometimes mentally pick their partners apart—they may look for all the reasons why this wouldn't work out, almost as a defense mechanism, a way to reject before being *rejected*. We can all pick up on that feeling of being "sized up" (this is why job interviews are particularly brutal) and it's an uncomfortable feeling we just want to get away from.

The men also often find these women a little *too* independent in that they feel like they would have nothing to offer. A guy definitely doesn't want to be a crutch or life-preserver, but he does want to feel like he brings something to the table, like he is adding to your life in some way. If you have it all figured out and can do it all on your own and don't need anything from anybody, then why would he want to be there?

If you find you're too picky, that you are always looking for something wrong with the people you date, that your relationships don't really go beyond a certain point, that guys seem to end things with you without any clear reasons why, then it's possible you have some emotional blockages you need to work through.

Did Sleeping With Him Too Soon Ruin The Relationship?

There is this long-standing idea that women are the gatekeepers of sex and men are the gatekeepers of commitment. And there is some truth there, but that doesn't mean you need to dangle sex in front of a man like holding a steak in front of a hungry tiger in order to keep him interested...and once he's fed, he'll be gone.

Some believe you need to wait a certain number or dates, others believe you need to wait until you've become official. But I believe that you can't set a universal standard for this sort of thing.

When it comes to sleeping with a guy, the number of dates is an arbitrary measure of the state of your relationship. What matters is the *quality* of the time you spend together. A girl who sleeps with a guy on the first date after an evening of intense, meaningful conversation that fosters a bond is much more likely to have a lasting relationship than a girl who sleeps with a guy on the fifth date when she hasn't really formed a connection with him.

The right time to sleep with a guy is when he's shown he's invested in you. (This is assuming you want a relationship with him. If you want a friend with benefits or steady booty call, then sleep with him whenever you want, just be safe!)

This doesn't necessarily mean he calls you his girlfriend or has said he loves you. It means you both are able to drop your masks and be real when you're together. It means he shares things with you he doesn't share with other people in his life (and vice versa). It means he cares about you and respects you as a person.

The fact is, men don't value what they perceive is readily and easily available to all other men.

When you sleep with a guy before you really know him, it's easy for him to assume that any other guy could have done it. When you sleep with him after getting to know who he truly is, he believes that you slept with him because of how amazing he is, and you wouldn't have chosen to sleep with just any other guy.

Guys appreciate women who are genuine and authentic, and you'd be surprised how easily a man can distinguish between a woman holding out to manipulate him into feeling what she wants him to feel, and a woman who holds out because she respects herself and is still trying to decide if this man is worth investing in any further.

Sex and relationships are two entirely different things for men; they don't necessarily see sex as a measure of the depth of the relationship the way most women do. For guys, sex is more of a reward for being in the relationship. Having sex with a guy is not enough to make him want to commit. Men do not get into relationships purely based on physical attraction, and a man wanting to sleep with you is not a measure of his actual *feelings* for you.

Before sleeping with him you have to understand that having sex with him will not guarantee a relationship or any sort of commitment. If that's what you're hoping for then you're setting yourself up to be greatly disappointed. It seems obvious yet so many women get tripped up in this area. Before sleeping with a guy you have to determine if he's interested in *you* or interested in having *sex with you*. The trouble is, it's not always easy to distinguish between these two vastly different things.

The right time to sleep with a guy is unique to every person and every relationship. You can't apply a three-date rule to every situation—only you know when the time is right. Sometimes it will be obvious, and other times you'll have to dig really deep to make sure you aren't deluding yourself.

If you genuinely care for him and know in your heart that he feels the same about you and you want to express your feelings in a physical way, then go for it. If you are unsure of how he feels, but are afraid he'll leave you if you don't put out, then please trust your gut and make sure you're putting yourself and your needs first.

When a man truly cares about you, you'll know because he'll show he cares about *you*. He'll make you a priority in his life, he'll want to get to know you (the *real* you), he'll bring you into his world and he'll want to be brought into yours, he'll put effort into the relationship, he'll commit to you. He won't just tell you he cares, he'll show it through his actions and he'll leave little room for doubt about how he truly feels. If you don't quite know where you stand yet, then wait a little longer. This is another way to see where he stands, because a guy who truly cares about you won't mind waiting.

Just be sure not to sleep with a guy for any of the following reasons:

> **You're afraid he's going to leave or lose interest.** First, it says something about the dynamic of the relationship if you're having these feelings, and you should spend time pondering why you feel this way. Is it insecurity? Is he not treating you right? Does he feel confused by your decision to hold out because he thinks sex is the expected next step? Whatever the reason, don't have sex with him if you're doing it in a bid to keep him around or interested.

He's pressuring you. Never ever have sex because you feel pressured. This is where personal boundaries come into play. If you aren't ready then you aren't ready. Don't apologize for it, don't make excuses for it, don't justify yourself to make him feel better. If he can't handle it, then that's his problem, not yours.

To deepen the relationship. Sex will not deepen your bond or connection if it isn't there before the sex. A man will not fall in love with you because you slept with him, nor will the act make him realize that he wants to commit himself to you. Giving a man great sex will never be enough to inspire him to commit. Men commit and fall in love for reasons that are completely separate from sex.

To prove he likes you or to feel desired. A man can have sex with a woman he hates as long as he's attracted to her... and even if he isn't—as they say, everyone's a supermodel in the dark. A man having sex with you does not say anything about whether or not he likes you. Does it mean he desires you? Yes. But using sex as a means for validation and to feel desired points to much deeper issues that need to be addressed. Of course, everyone likes to be wanted and desired. However, you should never sleep with a man to feel validated. When you sleep with a guy it causes the release of certain hormones like oxytocin that make you feel even more close and connected to him. If your relationship isn't established, then you might have a hard time distinguishing between intimacy in the bedroom and emotional intimacy, and this just opens the doors wide for hurt and disappointment.

With all relationship issues, the best advice is to love and respect yourself, know your worth, and work constantly on being the best version of yourself. When you place a high value on yourself, the world will follow suit. And when you value yourself enough to work on yourself, you will get to know yourself and will be more aware of your needs and desires. Ultimately you will have the strength and clarity to get what you truly want. More on this in the next chapter, so keep going!

Remember this: There are many ways to ruin a relationship and push him away, but they are all essentially caused by one thing: a lack of self-esteem. When you don't love yourself, you won't fully believe someone else can love you, and this can lead you to push love away even though it's the very thing you crave.

CHAPTER 6

Good Relationships Start With You

"The love you feel in life is a reflection of the love you feel in yourself." —*Deepak Chopra*

A successful relationship essentially comes down to two things: the right person at the right time. The first thing that's important to remember when it comes to relationships is that in general, like attracts like. That is, what you are or think you are is what you will attract.

If you don't value yourself, you will go for someone who doesn't treat you well and you will be OK with it because he's just validating how you feel about yourself. And this goes for all areas of your life: if you don't think you deserve it, you'll never have it. And if you get it, you'll always be afraid of losing it.

If you are emotionally unavailable, you will attract a guy who is emotionally unavailable, as we discussed in previous chapters. So it's crucial for you to become the kind of person you want to attract. It starts with you and becoming the best version of yourself.

Loving Yourself & Being More Confident

Good self-esteem attracts someone capable not only of healthy interactions but of loving you for who you are. If you're not sure of yourself inside, you'll seek validation outside.

Low self-esteem can prevent you from having the kind of love you want, and if you're in a relationship it can wreck the love you have. A romantic partner can certainly make you feel good, but they can never be the sole source of your self-esteem. If you don't already feel good about yourself, none of his compliments or caresses or demonstrations of love will have an impact, and you won't really be able to trust that he's genuine. It makes sense on a rational level, because how can you ever accept that someone else loves you if you don't already love yourself?

I just want to clarify what I mean by love yourself, lest I get accused of spreading toxic positivity. I don't mean love every single thing about yourself, I mean you can if you want to but that's not really a realistic goal. Also, loving yourself doesn't really have an end point, it's not like crossing the finish line of a marathon. It's not a linear journey, it will be up and down and it will last a lifetime. But when I say love yourself I really mean recognize you are *worthy* of love. That you are lovable. You embrace the good in you and accept the bad without shame or judgment. You accept that these are pieces of who you are and accept the entire picture.

The fact is, you can only let in as much love from the outside as you feel on the inside. If you don't feel good about yourself, you will never truly believe that someone else can love you. You will constantly be on the lookout for the other shoe to drop, for the guy you care about to leave, thus validating the "fact" that you are unworthy of love.

Self-esteem has significant, far-reaching ramifications for all areas of our lives. Building your sense of confidence and self-worth isn't always easy, but it can dramatically change your life for the better. **Here are some tips to get there:**

1. Stop Thinking Negative Thoughts

Negative thoughts are inevitable. Sometimes we keep them to ourselves and other times we lament out loud in hopes of getting some reassurance: "I'm so fat." "I'm so gross." "I'm never going to be successful." You know how the good old insecurity song and dance goes. Well from now on, stop entertaining these thoughts!

First you need to notice your thoughts. Just pay attention to them. Don't judge yourself for having the thought. Just notice it. Next, ask yourself: *Does this thought serve me well?*

So let's say you think, "I'm never going to find love. I'm going to end up alone." Ask yourself: *Does this thought serve me well?* And the answer: *No!*

If it doesn't feel good to think the thought then stop thinking the thought. Maybe it sounds simplistic, but I'm telling you, when you can master this it will *change your life*.

When thoughts that don't serve you pop up, just redirect your mind onto something else, preferably something positive and productive. Think about something you're excited about, think of something that brings you joy or a feeling of connection and fulfillment.

You can also try replacing the thought with the exact opposite. If you think, "I'm going to end up alone," say to yourself, "I will find the right person for me when the time is right."

You can do this with anything. If you're feeling drained and think, "I'm so tired," replace the thought with, "I feel energized!" (I personally do this one a lot as a mom of three little kids!)

Thoughts are real forces, and they have a huge impact on your mood and mindset. When you're thinking negative thoughts, you are creating a self-fulfilling prophecy. The good news is that you can control the thoughts that enter your mind, and you don't have to pay attention to the negative ones. Every thought resonates through your mind and body and creates a vibration, which will make those thoughts a reality. If you don't want to have a bad day or feel bad about yourself, then start thinking great thoughts!

2. Figure Out What Confidence Looks Like

It doesn't matter what other people think of you, it's the thoughts you have about yourself that make all the difference. If you want to be more confident, then make a list that details what confidence looks like and act accordingly. If you want to try out a bold look but feel hesitant, tell yourself, "A confident person doesn't care what other people think, and I'm a confident person and I like this outfit so I'll wear it!"

If you're afraid of approaching a guy because you're scared he'll reject you, say to yourself, "A confident person doesn't fear rejection because a confident person knows she's fabulous and a catch in every sense, and whoever doesn't see that is missing out. I am a confident person and I will be satisfied if this guy responds well to me, but it won't affect me if he doesn't."

If a guy is taking forever to text back and you start to panic, tell yourself, "A confident person doesn't stress over whether a guy will text back, she assumes he will, because why wouldn't he? She doesn't really care if he never resurfaces because if he doesn't, that's his loss." You get the idea. It may feel weird, or maybe like you're being delusional, but trust me, in time you will no longer be acting like a confident person, you will be one.

3. Find Your Own Happiness

Having a significant other is a wonderful thing, but it isn't the *only* thing and it certainly doesn't make you complete or give you happiness. If you don't have a special someone in your life, that's OK. It can actually be great because you get to be totally selfish and live life only for you. Think of it as a season. Right now you're in your single season, and seasons don't last forever. So make the most of it, because when it's over, it's over and you can never get this time back.

Before you can be happy with someone else, you truly need to find happiness within yourself. We are all wonderful, amazing creatures, and given that we certainly do not need a man to mirror this right back to us.

Happiness doesn't just happen, it's a choice you make and something you have to work on every day. It's far too easy to get caught up in everything that's wrong in your life, and it takes a bit of practice to train yourself to look at what's going right.

Negative thoughts seldom come one at a time. The minute you start focusing on one thing that's going wrong, all you'll see is everything that's wrong. And if you're one of the many women who think she'll be happy as soon as she's in a relationship...stop! Relationships do not lead to happiness and being single does not lead to a life of misery. The right relationship can certainly enhance your overall feelings of happiness, but it can never fill a void for you. Happiness *always* comes from within.

If I'm being totally honest, I am not a naturally happy person. Sadness just feels more comfortable and natural to me, and it's so, so easy for me to just slip back into that state the minute something goes even slightly wrong. I have to fight for my happiness every single day. It's a choice you have to make, a choice comprised of a lot of tiny choices that make up the sum of your day. So choose it. What time do you wake up in the morning? What do you do first? Where do you go? Who do you spend your time with? How do you structure your day? What do you prioritize? This is where your happiness is rooted.

Trust me, you can do it. You can get there. Instead of wasting your mental energy wondering why you don't have what you want, focus on creating a life that you love right now. Focus on what you can do today to enhance your feelings of happiness.

4. Stay Connected To Your Essence

We all have that one thing that makes us feel alive, that thing that makes us connected to our core. For me it's writing. Even though sometimes it's a struggle to put pen to paper, when I get in that zone there is nothing like it. I feel laser-focused and all my other needs melt away. On days when I really dedicate myself to writing and produce a lot, I feel amazing. I feel on top of the world. I feel energized and inspired and charged up, and that carries over into the rest of my day and makes me more productive in all areas. I'm also happier and in a better mood.

I know people who feel the same way when they paint or draw or dance or sing or exercise or cook or travel or go to museums or give advice. We all have that one thing that gives us a sense of accomplishment, a sense of purpose. Whatever that is for you, go after it. It won't always be easy, there will be times when you're too stressed or tired or busy. But make an effort to make the time, even if it's only for ten minutes a day.

Another exercise to help you tap into yourself is to visualize what your perfect day looks like. Picture it from start to finish. What time do you wake up? What do you do first? Who do you spend time with? Where do you go? What do you do?

After you map out this perfect day, try to incorporate elements of it into your daily life. Unfortunately it's not realistic for most of us to live our ideal day every single day, but you can bring in some elements of it. Maybe it means waking up an hour earlier to meditate or do yoga. Maybe it means going out of your comfort zone and trying something new. Whatever it is, make time for it. This is an active process; you have to make the time because time isn't going to just open itself up to you.

5. Try This Self-Love Exercise

Most people can't just know something intellectually; we need to feel it emotionally to really *know it*. This is why so many people have a hard time giving up smoking. Intellectually we all know the risks (and if you were unaware, it says it right there on the box: smoking kills!). Telling smokers the facts doesn't usually have an impact; you have to get to the emotional core of why they smoke.

Now in relationships, why would you need your partner to keep telling you he loves you? This knowledge was established the first time he said it. It's not like the people in a couple are learning something new every time the other person says, "I love you."

Imagine if after your boyfriend told you he loves you for the first time he said, "OK, glad we established that. I'll be sure to let you know if anything changes." I don't think you'd be too thrilled because the reason you want him to keep saying the words is not to know it, it's to *feel it*.

Every time he says it, you feel it. The reason you feel it is because you associate those words with all the things he's done to make you feel loved throughout the course of the relationship.

In order to really know anything, you have to feel it. This is true of just about everything in life.

When it comes to developing confidence and self-love, telling yourself over and over "I have self-love" won't work, and neither will keeping a running tab of your attributes or blowing kisses to yourself in the mirror.

Sure it's nice to be aware of all the wonderful things that make you, *you*, but telling yourself "I'm smart, I'm beautiful, I'm caring, I'm fun" isn't enough to firmly ingrain these beliefs into your psyche.

And if you aren't firm in these convictions, you become susceptible to questioning yourself when something happens that doesn't align with these notions (not getting attention from men, your boyfriend acting flaky, someone undermining you, etc.)

To experience feeling whole and complete, you need to feel the things that you already know.

A while back I learned this exercise from a teacher who has done extensive work in the field of psychology, and I put my own spin on it. A lot of my readers gave it a try and experienced amazing, almost life-changing results. So here it is:

Take a piece of paper and write Self-Love in the middle. Then around it write down 5-10 instances when you experienced love.

They can be times when you did something kind for someone else, moments when you felt proud of yourself, times when you felt completely content and secure with yourself or any time that you gave or received love.

You can also jot down quotes or song lyrics about love that strike a chord with you or times when you witnessed selfless love in its purest form.

Once you have a list, meditate on these memories. Close your eyes and allow your mind to reflect on each memory or idea. Paint a picture of the scene; see yourself and how you felt in that moment. If it's a quote or song lyric, reflect on the meaning of the words and try to paint a picture of what that idea would look like.

The second your mind starts to wander, think about the next example. Keep going until you've experienced all of them (take about 5-10 minutes to do this).

The mind is a tricky thing because it doesn't want to focus on a single topic for more than a few seconds. By creating images and letting your mind move from one instance to the next, you will maintain an unbreakable concentration.

As you go deeper, you will actually feel the positive emotions. When done right, this exercise is incredibly powerful and transformative.

In general, nothing anyone says or does actually has the power to affect your mood and your opinion of yourself unless you let it. If you're unsure of yourself, you'll be a lot more likely to allow the negativity to penetrate.

When you form the foundation of self-love, however, nothing on the outside can get you down.

When you know and feel with every fiber of your being how incredible you truly are, you will never again be at the mercy of someone else.

If your significant other acts in a way you don't understand or appreciate, you won't fall into despair. You'll realize that his actions have nothing to do with you and are no reflection of your inherent value and worth.

Why Confidence Matters In A Relationship

Now that we've discussed ways to increase your self-confidence, let's look at why it matters and how it makes a difference in your relationship. Healthy self-esteem is a prerequisite for healthy relationships. From my personal experiences and my years spent as a relationship writer and coach, I've learned that poor self-esteem is the number one cause of unhealthy relationships and the top relationship killer (not to mention life-ruiner overall).

Self-esteem isn't an essential need like food or water, but it's a supplement that can either dramatically improve your life or keep you stunted and unfulfilled.

Poor self-worth is what sabotages new relationships, traps us in bad relationships, and causes us to feel so devastated and broken when a relationship ends. And it poisons basically every other aspect of our lives. It's hard to truly enjoy anything when you feel terribly about yourself and who you are.

Having high self-esteem doesn't guarantee a happy relationship, but it does equip you with the skills to identify what you want and realize you deserve to get it, and the strength to walk away if something falls short. **Here are ten things people with high self-esteem do differently in their relationships:**

1. Confident People Don't Analyze Whether Or Not Someone Likes Them—They Assume They Do

People with high self-esteem believe they are worthy of love and don't question how someone feels about them. They know that they are good, competent, and lovable, and trust that the right person for them will see this. They don't attach their worth to what a guy thinks, and as a result they don't feel stressed and anxious when a guy's feelings are unclear. Instead, they assume he likes them and they're able to be present in the relationship and enjoy it without being weighed down by fears and doubts.

2. Confident People Realize That When A Relationship Falls Apart It's Because It Wasn't Right, Not Because They Did Something Wrong

Not everyone is a match; sometimes two people are just incompatible and this doesn't make either of them flawed or bad. Confident women don't take it personally when a guy doesn't want a romantic relationship. They realize that it must not be the right match and they move on with their sense of self firmly intact.

But when a girl is insecure and a guy leaves, she spirals. She may obsess, analyze, and replay every interaction in an attempt to uncover what she did wrong. She may know on a conscious level that it simply wasn't a match, but deep down she holds on to the destructive belief that she was the problem...she was unlovable and this guy and all other guys she wants will never want her back.

3. Confident People Set Healthy Boundaries

Healthy personal boundaries and high self-esteem go hand in hand. Having strong boundaries means you prioritize your needs and your emotions and do not assume responsibility for someone else's needs and emotions.

Confident women know what they will and will not accept and don't allow themselves to be pressured or guilted into doing things they don't want to do. They act in accordance with who they are and what they believe and don't tailor their behavior for a guy, or do things solely to keep him interested and happy. When you have weak boundaries, you may sell yourself out in a relationship and put up with treatment that you know objectively is unacceptable.

A woman with healthy boundaries will not lose herself in a relationship and will not allow her identity to be contingent upon how a man sees her. She will continue to maintain her own life outside of the relationship without giving up her friends, hobbies, or alone time. She won't abandon important parts of herself or her life for the sake of the relationship. She brings her fully formed self into the relationship, and if the guy wants something else, or something more that she doesn't have to offer, she will leave.

4. Confident Women Trust Themselves And The Decisions They Make

A key component of having high self-esteem is trusting yourself to make the right choices while also realizing you are well equipped to cope should things go awry. People with high self-esteem don't constantly question their actions or feel conflicted about the right thing to say or do. They act on how they feel and are comfortable being their true, authentic selves.

People with low self-esteem don't trust their judgment, don't trust their gut instincts, and are afraid of being wrong. As a result, they either live their lives in a constant state of anxiety or they depend completely on others to guide them along the right path. This obviously does not do much to help one's sense of autonomy, which is also a key element of healthy self-esteem.

5. Confident People Don't Show Off Or Talk Themselves Up

Confident people don't need to tell the world how great they are. Only insecure people secretly feel that they are unworthy and feel the need to hide this by bragging about their achievements or talking themselves up.

A woman who reveals herself gradually, carefully peeling back layers of herself over time, is significantly more attractive than a woman who lays it all out there. When you feel that you are worthy, you don't need to tell people...they just know. A big mistake insecure women make in the early stages of dating is trying to sell themselves to a guy. This can be completely innocent, but it comes from a deeper sense of insecurity and inadequacy. Confident women don't need to sell themselves; rather, they use dating as a means to determine which guys are worthy of *their* time and affection.

6. Confident People Accept Responsibility

Confident people accept responsibility for their actions and emotions. They don't blame or shame others if they feel unhappy and don't accuse them of "making" them feel a certain way. They don't blame men for being jerks and they don't view themselves as the victims of other people and circumstances.

They realize that their time is their responsibility. As a result, they don't wait around in dead-end relationships, hoping something will magically change, and they don't blame their exes for wasting their time. They take responsibility for their choices, both good and bad, and use mistakes as opportunities to grow and become even better.

7. Confident People Take The Relationship For What It Is And Don't Need It To Be A Certain Way

Confident people feel secure in their relationships. They don't need to have a title or a ring as some sort of confirmation that the guy cares. They are able to just be present and in the relationship and let it unfold organically, without force or pressure. This is not to say they stay with guys who won't commit and are all cool and go-with-the-flow about it. If a guy can't commit in the way they want, then they'll move on. They are able to give and receive freely in their relationships and as a result, they don't stress out about labels. They just know that if it's right, it will work out. And if it's not right, they'll move on.

8. Confident People Don't Stay In Bad Relationships

Confident people do not stay in relationships where they don't feel respected, appreciated, and valued. And they don't assume all the blame if a relationship isn't working and take it upon themselves to try to solve the problem by giving and doing more. They aren't afraid to walk away, and the thought that they won't be able to find something better or that they will wind up alone doesn't cross their minds. They can quickly see when a situation is damaging and will remove themselves immediately.

Only insecure people put up with treatment that is unacceptable, in large part because they feel on some level that that's what they deserve. When you learn to value yourself, you will weed out anyone who doesn't truly value you.

9. Confident People Don't Desperately Seek Reassurance

People with high self-esteem know they are loved and lovable. They don't need a guy to remind them every day–it's just something they feel and know. When you are insecure you need constant validation and will become resentful if your partner doesn't give it to you. You'll blame him for "making you" feel insecure or unloved in the relationship. You may work harder to try to please him and earn his love, or you may withhold your love and affection to even the score. This insecurity manifests as neediness: you *need* constant reassurance, and if you don't get it you lash out and blame your partner for not providing it.

The fact is, if you don't feel good about yourself, nothing he does will ever be enough. If you don't truly believe you're worthy of love, you will never believe someone can love you. What happens is the relationship becomes a battle of wills: you fight for validation, he retreats because he feels pressured and suffocated, you view his retreat as a sign he doesn't love you and you fall into despair, he resents that nothing he does is good enough and resents the fact that you don't trust how he feels and so he stops trying, you see this as further proof he doesn't care...and either the relationship ends or continues to make you both miserable indefinitely.

Again, this isn't just a relationship thing. If you're insecure, you'll seek reassurance everywhere. You will need it from your boss or co-workers, you will need it every time you post something on social media. You will need it from your friends. You basically don't feel good or worthy or smart or attractive or anything really unless people on the outside are constantly reflecting this back at you.

10. Confident People Choose Wisely

Confident people use their head and heart when choosing a romantic partner. They are able to quickly assess if someone is emotionally healthy and can give them what they need in a relationship. They don't let their ego get too intertwined with their emotions and they make sure they are fundamentally compatible with someone before they get too involved.

As we discussed: *like attracts like*. A confident person will attract another confident person. An insecure person will unconsciously seek out relationships with men who are insecure and who will make them feel more insecure. They will want the unavailable guys, the guys who can't commit, the guys who have walls up. These are the ones they will feel infatuated by, not the ones who show real, genuine interest. Oftentimes this happens because on an unconscious level, the insecure girl feels that if she can break through his walls, or get him to change his ways, *then* she'll really be worthy and valuable. This never, ever works. Instead, she just ends up compromising her integrity even further by chasing the relationship.

If you don't value yourself, then you will always be attracted to people who don't value you either. Confident people value and accept themselves for who they are. They embrace the good and are accepting of the not-so-good. As a result, they attract quality partners and are able to connect on a real, genuine level, one that leads to true intimacy and a healthy relationship.

Why Does The Woman Have To Change To Make A Relationship Work?

By now, female readers might be thinking: *Why is it always the woman's fault? Why do I have to do all this work to have a loving relationship?*

Over the years, many readers have said things along the lines of:

> "Why can't he just accept me as I am? Why do I have to change?"
>
> "Why don't you tell this stuff to men?"
>
> "Why do I need to change anything? He should be the one to change!"
>
> "It's not fair, he acts like a jerk and I have to be the one to work on myself?"

The easiest answer to these questions is: *you* are the only person you have complete control over. And it's not a woman thing, I give the exact same advice to men.

You can try forcing your man to change, but I guarantee it won't work. Instead, you will most likely find yourself alone.

The truth is, the way you act has a major impact over the way the other person responds. As a result, learning how to modify your behavior (and this does not mean turning into someone else, it just means acting in accordance with your best and highest self) can lead to a much better, much happier, much more fulfilling relationship...and isn't that the ultimate goal here? And it goes without saying that you already chose a good, stable, emotionally healthy partner, as we discussed in the first chapter.

The point is not to place blame, but to take responsibility for what we bring into our interactions, whether in romantic relationships, friendships, work relationships, or with family.

I focus a lot on the importance of changing your mindset—which, in turn, changes your behavior—because these things can ultimately change your life and your relationships for the better...as long as you can see the bigger picture without getting frustrated by the effort you will need to exert.

The way you think affects not only you and your self-esteem, it can have a big impact on the people around you.

Just look at your own life for proof. When you're in a good place, things typically will go your way.

When you're in a bad place, things often go from bad to worse—you get into arguments with your friends, you're distracted at school or work and miss important deadlines, you yell at your boyfriend for something stupid, you stub your toe on a very heavy door.

When we have complaints, we usually don't realize how we might be causing the problems ourselves. It starts by looking deep within yourself and figuring out what place you're coming from. And asking the hardest question of all: *How am I responsible for the things that happen to me?* Eek. Personal responsibility is not for the faint of heart. It's just so much easier to blame other people, to blame our circumstances, to blame anything and everything except ourselves.

We need to take responsibility for how we show up in a relationship.

When you come from a place of ego/insecurity/fear, it can cause another person to feel attacked, and when people feel attacked they will immediately go on the defensive.

For instance, if you complain to your partner that he's never there for you or that he's acting cold or distant, he will be put on the defensive. He will perceive that you don't appreciate him and will act even more distant. Also, if he feels like you're blaming or attacking him, it will block him from being the great partner that he can be.

When you're in a good place, you will be more able to speak with thoughtfulness and compassion. This will usually awaken the same value system in others, and they will be more likely to give you what you want.

We all have egos to protect. When you criticize harshly, it rarely inspires people to be better. It just puts them on the defensive and makes them inclined to point out your faults, too.

The good news is we all have an innate desire to be our best selves. When you can come from a place of confidence, understanding, and just the right amount of compassion, you will inspire the other person to bring his best self to the table, too, the side that wants to do good and reach its ultimate potential.

Becoming aware of your own sensitivities can make you aware of what a gift it is to inspire someone to be his best self, rather than trying to force it to happen through criticism.

What does this look like in relationships? It comes down to recognizing and appreciating the other person for who he is and not placing demands on him that stem from your own insecurities.

It entails being in a good place emotionally, because when you bring your best to a relationship, most relationship problems solve themselves.

The worst thing you can do when you're unhappy in your relationship is blame the other person for *making* you feel a certain way. It may be the easier option, but it certainly isn't the most effective.

If there are problems, the best thing you can do is look within yourself and see how you can be better, both in the relationship and overall. If you're bringing your best to the table but problems persist, then it might be time to assess whether this is a relationship you want to continue.

Again, I'm not saying your partner should sit back while you do all the work. Both people need to put in effort to be their best selves so that they can have the best possible relationship. The reason I'm directing my advice to you, not him, is because, well, you're the one reading this book!

Why You Feel Empty

By now you know the gist: the key to a happy relationship and a happy life is finding fulfillment within yourself. That's what makes you interesting and engaging. That's what makes people drawn to you. But what if you can't get there? What if you feel perpetually empty?

If you do, you're not alone. Most people struggle with feelings of emptiness, numbness, and isolation that they can't shake. For some, it's fleeting. For others, it's constant.

A lot of people play the "as soon as" game.

I'll feel fulfilled as soon as I have X amount of money, as soon as I lose X amount of weight, as soon as I get my dream job, as soon as I buy a home, as soon as I have a boyfriend, and on and on. We can spend a lifetime chasing the "as soon as".

So let's look at the most common reasons you may feel lonely or empty because you can't solve a problem unless you know what the problem is.

1. Your Life Is Unbalanced

Balance is the key to a happy, fulfilled life. That means you make time for different areas that are important to you: time to take care of yourself, time to spend with friends, time to do something meaningful or pursue your passion.

Most people feel empty when their life skews too far in one direction, like when all they do is work and they're too exhausted to do anything else. Or a stay at home mom who is *only* with her kids and doesn't have time for friends or even herself. Or someone who abandons all other aspects of their life once they're in a relationship and focuses solely on that.

There is a lot that needs to get done in a day and there never seems to be enough time so you will have to be clever and creative in your rearranging but it can be done. You only get one life, so make the most of it!

2. You Don't Really Know Who You Are

You can't really know what fulfills you if you don't even have a grasp on who you are. And a lot of people have no idea who they truly are. We live in a weird time of social isolation and social media overload and it's hard to know who we truly are deep down. And even people who do know who they are can lose touch with themselves from time to time.

Most people just keep going going going and don't pause to think and reflect.

Knowing who you are will anchor you in life. When you don't know who you are, you might feel aimless or like you're running on autopilot.

Or maybe you get into the toxic habit of defining yourself according to your job, your status, your relationship. Maybe you lose yourself completely in relationships and just mold yourself into what you think the other person wants.

I see this happen a lot and it's devastating when these relationships fall apart because you don't have a true self to fall back on.

One great way to discover yourself is to journal. Look at the things that happen in your life and write out how you feel. It doesn't have to be beautiful prose, you're not trying to be published. Just let it rip and see what comes out. And check in with yourself. Ask yourself: *How did that experience make me feel? Would I want to do that again?* Look at what makes you excited, what makes you feel alive and connected...and do more of those things!

3. You Have Unresolved Trauma

This can be a traumatic childhood or a traumatic breakup and anything in between. It's way easier to run from the pain or numb the pain than it is to face it and deal with it.

But pain doesn't go away just because it goes unacknowledged. You can ignore those feelings as long as you'd like, but they will still be in there, and they will come exploding out seemingly out of nowhere. Maybe someone says something innocent and you feel irrationally angry. You're not angry at the person, these feelings come up because that person pressed on an unhealed wound.

We've all had that experience of becoming irrationally angry over something small. We know the emotion is real, we feel it, but we're not sure why it came forth with such roaring intensity. Well, that's usually your trauma talking.

And those feelings are going to stay buried within you and will cause this gnawing empty feelings until you face them.

4. You Don't Pursue Your Passions

You may not even know what your passions are, this ties into not knowing who you are.

It's really important to have meaningful goals and passions, and we all have them.

I remember finding mine. It was when I wrote my first e-book. I never felt more connected or more alive. I was barely sleeping because all I wanted to do was work and write. I felt like I transcended the human experience, I didn't need food (I did still force myself to eat, though!), I didn't need sleep, I didn't need people. I just needed to write.

Granted, this caused problems when the book was complete because my life was unbalanced and then I felt empty again and had to go back into a mode of creating a balanced life that involved more than just typing away, but I did discover that wow, I really, really enjoy writing!

So find your thing. Maybe your career is also your passion, or maybe you don't love your job and your passion is something else.

It could be cooking or painting or volunteering or learning an instrument or learning a new language or getting involved with a meaningful cause—find that thing that gives you a feeling of worth and passion.

5. You Don't Have Meaningful Relationships

When it comes to relationships, quality is so much more important than quantity. It is crucial to surround yourself with quality people who see you and love you for who you are.

And you have to nurture those relationships. It's so easy to get caught up in the grind of daily life, relationships take effort.

If all you have are superficial relationships, you will feel an emptiness because we are naturally social creatures, we're pack animals, we need our social tank to be full.

You may also desperately seek a romantic relationship to plug up this hole and then rely too much on your relationship to fill your social needs.

Or maybe you commit the cardinal sin of abandoning your friendships as soon as a guy enters the picture. I did this in my relationship with one of my exes and I remember when the relationship ended, I had no one to turn to and it was the most empty I had ever felt. In addition to working on getting over the breakup, now I also had to rebuild my friendships from the ground up.

6. Too Much Time On Social Media

Social media can sometimes (ok, maybe often) be absolute poison for our mental health. On the one hand, we know it's not real. On the other hand, it's hard not to look at these other people with their seemingly perfect lives and not feel like we're missing out or we're doing something wrong or we're not enough.

This is why I personally don't like following any perfectly curated accounts—yes, I like to follow people who inspire me, but also ones that are real, not always presenting the perfect facade.

Try to only follow accounts that make you feel inspired, not depressed or jealous and envious and angry.

And try to limit your time on social media if possible and do other things that make you feel good.

I also want to add that feeling empty can also be a symptom of a number of mental health conditions—depression, anxiety, bipolar, PTSD. If you suspect this is the case, then I would highly advise you see a mental health professional to get properly diagnosed so you can learn to manage whatever is going on. As Dr. Phil says, you can't change what you don't acknowledge.

Finding Your Own Happiness

I've already mentioned this several times, but it bears repeating: your happiness is essential, both to your overall well-being and to your love life. Happiness and self-esteem go hand in hand, so finding ways to live a happier life will increase your sense of self-worth.

One big mistake a lot of people make in relationships is expecting the other person to make them happy. It doesn't work that way.

In order to find true happiness in life, you need to work on yourself and make a few adjustments to the way you live your life. If you don't, you will find yourself repeating the same unhealthy patterns over and over again. As the famous quote by Pema Chodron goes: *Nothing ever goes away until it has taught us what we need to know.*

These tweaks are actually pretty simple and if you do them right, you will attain the kind of genuine happiness most people spend their whole lives pursuing.

1. Don't Rely On Other People To Make You Happy

Relying on other people to make you happy will leave you endlessly disappointed. The reason most people feel unhappy in their lives is they expect other people to give them things that they can only give themselves. Think about it—if you continually outsource the task of filling a void inside of you and finding happiness, you will never be fully satisfied; instead you'll be at the mercy of everyone you meet.

Only you can control how happy you are and how you feel about yourself. Stop blaming other people for "making" you feel a certain way. Put yourself in the driver's seat and accept responsibility for your own happiness and your own sense of self-worth. You have to choose happiness every single day; it's an active process.

2. Conquer Jealousy

Jealousy is one of the most destructive qualities a person can possess. In life you will inevitably come across people who are better looking, more successful, funnier, richer, etc., but who cares? I'm sure you have qualities that they're lacking. No good can ever come from envying what someone else has; it will just make you bitter and jaded.

Once upon a time people only had access to their immediate circles. You had your friends and your family and you could see what they wore, what their houses looked like, you knew where they went on vacation, but that was it. You probably didn't know things like their morning skincare routine, what they ate for every meal of the day, how organized their cabinets were, their supplement regimen, their makeup technique. And if you knew these things, it was on a "real" level. But now we know *all these things* about countless strangers on the internet and we're seeing it all presented in the most beautiful, filtered, perfectly curated light.

How can you not feel jealous and insecure? How can you not compare? It's really hard. And we all know it's the "highlight reel" of their lives but it doesn't matter, that's not how it *feels* when we see the images and instagram stories.

My advice is first be mindful of who you follow on social media. If an account makes you feel bad, don't follow them! Try to only follow accounts that make you feel good and inspired.

Also, when you feel jealous or envious, try to dig a little deeper and get to the root of it. What's bothering you exactly?

Let's say you see that a friend or just someone you follow got engaged and this make you jealous. Ask yourself why. And the answer will probably be: *I'm scared it won't happen for me.* Or maybe you feel frustrated seeing other people get something you'd desperately want. Now try to turn it around to something positive, "She found her match and someday I will find mine."

Also remember this: no one gets to have it all. Maybe you want some influencer's body or wardrobe, but do you want every other life circumstance of hers? Do you want to give up everything you have for everything she has? Probably not because no one has it all. No one has the perfect body and perfect partner and perfect children and perfect physical and mental health and perfect family and perfect upbringing and perfect ability to cope. No one. Not one person. Remember that.

3. Be Genuinely Happy For Other People

This is the opposite of being jealous. If people you know come upon some good fortune—an amazing job, an incredible guy, a huge raise—be happy for them.

I know I know I know. It's *so hard.* But remember: they didn't take anything away from you. Your friend getting engaged didn't take away your chances of ever being engaged. Someone getting a raise doesn't mean your salary won't ever increase as well.

Those people struggled just like most people do on the quest to get what they want. And if they didn't struggle in certain areas—maybe your best friend married the first guy she ever dated—then let me assure you, they've struggled in other areas because *no one gets to have it all.*

They put in the work they needed to and reaped a reward and the same can happen for you. Try not to let other people's good fortune become your misery. Instead redirect your mind to see it as motivation and inspiration for you to get what you want in life.

4. Be Nice To People

You know who's mean? Unhappy people, that's who. Happy people feel good about themselves and about life and want to make other people feel good as well. Doing acts of kindness actually causes a chemical reaction that makes you feel really good. You can do little things, like smiling at strangers or giving up your seat on the subway for an old lady, or big things like volunteer work. For extra credit, try not to talk negatively behind someone's back, or gossip. While it may seem fun, no one ever really feels good about bashing someone else.

5. Be Grateful

There's a saying that goes: *happiness isn't having what you want, but wanting what you have.* Most of us are trained to look at what's wrong in our lives rather than what's right. We yearn for a better job, a better relationship, better friends, a better body—we hone in on what's missing and overlook what's right there in front of us. Try to change your filter system and instead zoom in on things to be grateful for. I promise you'll find them if you look. I can also guarantee that there are many people out there praying for things you take for granted every single day.

These days everyone is buzzing about manifestation. And it's a great idea—you can have anything you want if you just dream it into existence. If you're into this idea, I'm sure you've heard of the abundance mindset which essentially translates to being grateful. When you are grateful for what you have, you attract more abundance. When you focus on what you lack, you are in a scarcity mindset and you don't attract the things you want.

6. Accept That Which You Cannot Change

There are certain things you can't change. You can't change your upbringing, your height, your general appearance. You also can't change the past. All you can do is move forward and try not to repeat the same mistakes. Don't waste your energy thinking about what a crappy lot in life you got. Instead, focus on what you have and on how you can develop qualities that will allow you to reach your full potential.

Your circumstances are unique to you and have given you the tools you need to carve out your own unique path.

7. Do Something About That Which You *Can* Change

If you need to lose weight, hate your friends, are miserable at your job...do something about it! The surest way to feel good about yourself is to push yourself to go beyond what you thought you were capable of. Change isn't easy, but you only live once and no one is going to live your life for you. It's up to you to find the strength and motivation to take the steps to get what you want. Working towards a goal feels good. When you have that spark of feeling good and feeling accomplished, you'll want to do even more things that make you feel good and accomplished.

8. Let Go Of Grudges

We all know the saying: "Holding a grudge is letting someone live in your head rent free." When you hold grudges, you're only hurting yourself. You're allowing negativity to course through you, and you're keeping yourself stuck in a painful past. Forgive the people who have wronged you and just let it go. Maybe you think they don't deserve forgiveness. Fair enough. But trust me, harboring feelings of anger and resentment is punishing you more than it's punishing them, so what's the point?

9. Let The Chips Fall Where They May

It took me a long time to realize that the sky wouldn't fall if I personally wasn't holding it up, and it's a lesson that has changed my life! Most people can't enjoy their lives because they're so busy micromanaging every detail. Yes, there is a time to make things happen. There is also a time to just let things happen. Take a breath, loosen up your grip on life, and try to adopt a bit of a *laissez-faire* attitude. Trust that everything will be OK.

10. Watch The Company You Keep

Oprah once said "Surround yourself only with people who will lift you higher," and this is a mantra I stand by. The people in your life will inevitably have an impact on you. When it comes to friends, quality is always better than quantity. Weed out the negative people in your life who drag you down, and spend more time with positive, optimistic people who see the good in you and encourage you to be your best self.

11. Move Your Body

I know you've heard this one before, but you have to move! Get outside and take a walk everyday. Exercise, sweat, get those endorphins flowing. This will make you happy. This will make you feel good and accomplished. When you feel good, you want to do more things that make you feel good. Good habits attract more good habits, this can also be known as habit stacking and it's life-changing

12. Believe In Yourself

I'm sure you've heard this one too, but you need to hear it again! Believe in yourself, believe you can do it, believe you can and will have the life you want. Believe that it will happen in the right time. Believe that the universe isn't out to get you, it's serving you. All the pain and problems you've endured are part of the journey to take you where you are meant to go.

Do you know the number one factor that determines success? It's not your IQ, it's *grit*. Grit is having passion and perseverance for your goals. It essentially comes down to *knowing you can do it*. And you'll probably fail a few times. But when you have grit, you don't give up.

You don't give up on love because it hasn't worked out for you yet. You don't give up on pursuing your dream job because thus far you've only faced rejection. You don't give up on training for the marathon even though it's *really* hard because you know you can do it.

13. Get More Sleep

So simple, yet so hard to put into practice! We have shows to binge, social media platforms to scroll, we don't want the day to end and to start all over again. But if you start to prioritize sleep, even just going to bed a half hour earlier every night, it will change your life! It has also been scientifically proven that people who get enough sleep are significantly happier[2], so make this a priority!

14. Surround Yourself With Inspiration

Read inspiring books or articles, follow inspiring social media account, listen to inspiring podcasts. There are so, *so* many resources out there. Try to slot in some time every day, even if it's ten minutes in the morning while you're making your coffee, to absorb something inspiring and motivational.

Remember this: You have a lot more power over your life than you realize. A good, loving, healthy, happy relationship starts with you, and the better place you're in emotionally, the better your relationship (and life) will be. So do whatever you need to do to get there!

CHAPTER 7

How to Be Good at Relationships (& Stop Stressing Over Them!)

"Love is the condition in which the happiness of another person is essential to your own." —*Robert Heinlein*

I know it may not seem this way, but relationships are actually surprisingly simple. A lot of women approach romantic relationships like a game of chess. They plot and strategize and worry that one wrong move will ruin everything and cost them the game. But you don't need to follow a stringent playbook to get a loving relationship. You don't need to become someone you're not, or act in a way that isn't true to who you are.

What it really comes down to is becoming your best self while also developing an awareness and understanding of what it takes to have an amazing, loving, mutually fulfilling relationship. What it *actually* takes, not the idealized fantasy that so many have come to view as a reality.

Four Basic Rules To Get The Love You Never Thought You Could Have

If you can master a few basic principles about relationships and what it takes to have the *right* relationship, you will overcome confusion and heartbreak and effortlessly get the relationship you've always wanted.

Whether you're in a relationship or single, here are the top four rules to live by to get the love you want:

1. Never Want Someone Who Doesn't Want You

Sounds obvious, but sadly, it's not! When it comes to relationships, we can delude ourselves in some pretty impressive ways. We find signs to prove that things are the way we want them to be and that he feels the way we want him to feel.

Now here's the truth of the matter. If a guy says or indicates he wants to be with you, but isn't actually *with you* for whatever reason (*I don't like labels...my ex-girlfriend was evil...I'm stressed about my job...my dog died...etc.*), then don't waste your time. Don't help his case by reasoning and rationalizing why his excuses make sense (but he is *really* busy! And his last girlfriend sounds like *such* a nightmare, and his dog was his *best friend*).

When someone is giving you excuses for why he can't do something, what he's really doing is telling you he doesn't *want* to do it. Some reasons may be quite impressive and there may even be sprinkles of truth mixed in there, but when it comes down to it, if he wants to be with you, he will be. Are there exceptions? Yes, but they are very, very rare. And even if a guy can't commit for whatever reason, he will still make sure to let you know he's invested in a real and substantial way.

If a guy isn't showing you that he is committed and that he wants to be with you and only you, then stop wanting that from him. It isn't easy, but it's a far better alternative than wasting months or even years of your life waiting around for some guy to get his act together, wouldn't you agree?

2. Choose Someone Who Brings Out The Best In You

Being in a relationship shouldn't be your end goal, the end goal should be attaining the *right* relationship.

When two people are in a relationship, they should bring out the best in one another. They should challenge each other to grow so that their best attributes strengthen and they become the best versions of themselves. Bringing out the best doesn't mean you are your best possible self at all times, that's just not realistic. It comes from being fully seen and accepted for who you are. This type of relationship gives you the space to grow in an important way.

When a relationship crushes you and leaves you feeling paranoid, anxious, insecure, inadequate, and always on edge, just waiting for the other shoe to drop, you're cheating yourself out of having the immense benefits a good relationship can provide.

So many of my readers and coaching clients feel miserable and trapped by their relationships. Yet despite these agonizing feelings of hurt/despair/insecurity/fear, they are unable to extricate themselves from the situation because of their all-consuming feelings for the other person.

They get so caught up in their feelings for him, or his presumed feelings for them, that they miss the most important variable in the equation. And that is: do I like myself when I'm with this person?

I've been in relationships where I almost didn't recognize myself, ones where my flaws were magnified and my good attributes were tucked away somewhere beyond reach. It's a miserable feeling, one that can have lasting ramifications long after the relationship (inevitably) ends.

At the end of the day, you are all you have. You need to be your greatest ally in the world. You need to do what's best for you and what will make you happy and help you reach your potential. If your relationship is sending you in the opposite direction, stop wasting your strength and energy on making it work and instead use that energy to walk away.

3. Take Responsibility

We all need to take responsibility for how we show up in a relationship. And here is something I want to hammer in: Your time is *your* responsibility.

If you are dating the undateable, then you can't really be upset when it doesn't work out. If you choose to stay with a guy who won't commit, then you can't really blame him when you wake up one day and realize you've been living in a dead-end relationship for the last few months or years.

You need to take ownership of your choices and your role in a relationship and your life. What role do you play? Are you the tragic victim, always at the mercy of others? Or are you the triumphant heroine? You get to decide.

Being bitter and angry and jaded won't help you. Yes, I know what it's like to be betrayed and hurt and disappointed. I know all the negative feelings, I lived with them in agonizing pain for too much of my life. But you don't need to live there. You can rewrite the script. You can be the heroine. You just need to stop blaming everyone else and look at yourself.

If you were in a toxic relationship, ask yourself: *How did I also contribute to this toxicity?* (Notice I said *also*, I'm not blaming you. I know there was a lot more at play). Look inward. That's how you grow. Instead of asking why did he do this to me, ask yourself: *why did I do this to me? Why did I stay when I knew better?*

Facing yourself isn't easy, but when you do, that's when those knots start to loosen, that's when you begin to heal, and that's when you're ready to be in a healthy relationship.

4. Be A Chooser

This is a really important mindset shift to have when dating. You need to exercise your power of choice. Most women don't do this with a guy they really like. Instead, they get stuck plotting and planning their every move in an effort to prove their worth to him. This is the *worst* way to be in a relationship. For one, it reeks of insecurity and neediness. It also puts the guy in the driver's seat and essentially tells him he can dictate the terms of the relationship. When this happens, you'll find yourself in a situation with a guy who will essentially do whatever he wants because he knows he can get away with it and you'll still be there.

Being a chooser isn't so much a set of behaviors as it is a state of mind. The mentality is one that asks: Is *he* good enough for *me*? Of all the guys I could have, is he the one I choose? The opposite of this is thinking, "He's out of my league, I really hope he doesn't lose interest. What can I do to win him over and get him to choose me?"

What About Playing Games & The Chase?

By now we know that having an amazing relationship essentially comes down to being your most amazing version of you. (And choosing wisely, of course!) But you may be wondering about the chase...haven't we always been told it's essential? I get asked about it constantly because it's something that has been so firmly drummed into our minds.

Women who are good at the chase aren't necessarily good at relationships; they're just good at getting guys to chase them. I know this all too well because I used to be one of those girls, I could hook 'em and reel 'em in, but I couldn't quite keep them. Learning how to be good at relationships goes far beyond learning how to get guys to pursue you. (Although this is important to a degree, as you'll see.)

So what's the deal? Do you need to play games to get the guy?

I have a friend I jokingly refer to as my biggest muse because this girl simply refuses to learn her lesson when it comes to men and relationships.

I try and I try to break things down for her, but she continues to make the same mistakes. While it provides me with tons of stories to use as illustrations of what *not* to do, I really wish she would take my advice a little more seriously. But if she won't, hopefully you will.

So here's the latest installment of the drama in her love life. She was dating a guy for a year who refused to call her his girlfriend, giving her some song and dance about not liking labels and having commitment issues, yada yada yada.

After endless urging from me, she finally put her foot down and said she didn't want to be in this relationship no-man's-land anymore and wanted a commitment.

It's very difficult to break a relationship pattern that is firmly established (in this case he had enjoyed the benefits of having a girlfriend without the responsibility of being in a relationship for over a year), and she knew that the chances of him doing a total turnaround on the spot were slim. But she was also sick of not being "enough" for him and knew something had to be done.

The conversation went pretty much as I predicted: he still refused to commit and they ultimately decided to take a "break."

Against my advice, she texted him several times during this break. While he would respond, his responses were pretty short and vague. I finally had to get a little harsher with her and tell her how desperate she was making herself look by constantly reaching out. If a girl is confident, loves her life, and respects herself, she will never need to play a single game. She won't pretend she doesn't have time for a guy who doesn't prioritize her; she will inherently busy herself with other things and move past him.

She won't be obsessed with trying to win over some guy who doesn't treat her right to begin with, she will skeptically give him another shot (and only if he proves himself deserving of it) and then will assess him to decide if he's worth her time.

She won't all of a sudden see a guy as soon as he decides he wants to see her. She will realize she has the power to choose and will not reduce herself to the role of waiting to be chosen.

She sees the bigger picture and isn't ruled by what she wants in the present moment.

For instance, even though she may really want a guy and truly care for him, she realizes that giving in and accepting less than what she needs won't get her what she wants in the end (a committed relationship). It would only give her the temporary satisfaction of being with him in the moment while giving way to more confusion and doubts the next day.

She can hold herself back without being afraid that the guy will move on because she isn't worth pursuing.

Whenever I would tell my friend to hold back and not respond, she would usually say "But what if he never comes back?" And she would say it with such fear in her voice, like it was the worst possible outcome she could imagine. She didn't believe she was worth fighting for. Sadly, this is a faulty mindset a lot of us may unknowingly have.

Self-fulfilling prophecies are real and powerful. If you don't believe you're worthy, you won't be. I mean, how can you expect others to believe something about you that you don't even believe about yourself? The truth is, a lot of women lack confidence and strength, and it's not something that can be gained overnight.

It takes time and it takes work. In the meantime, you have to act as if you are the person you want to be. And this is where "games" come in.

Ideally, acting like a confident, secure woman will turn you into one.

Here is how human beings operate (this goes for all areas of life, not just relationships). When we work for something, we come to appreciate its value and will invest in it more. The more we invest in something the more we come to care about it, and the more we care about it the harder we'll work to hold onto it.

A friend of mine recently met a great guy at a party. He called her two days later asking her out, and she came to me in a panic the minute they got off the phone, saying: "What do I do? How should I act on the date? Are there any rules I'm supposed to be following? I really like him and I don't want to mess this up!"

This is the absolute worst mindset to have before a date. In this scenario, she's making him the prize that she needs to win over. She's worried about saying or doing something to turn him off and cause him to realize what she already believes to be true...that she's not good enough.

When you have this attitude, the message you're sending to the guy is: *I'm unworthy of you, but I hope that if I try hard enough to please you, you'll overlook that fact and choose me anyway.* Is that who you want to be? The 'please pick me' girl? I thought not.

I know it's easier said than done, but you have to turn the tables and see yourself as the catch, as the one with the power to choose.

If you can genuinely come from this place, you'll never have to strategize in a relationship. Stop worrying so much about how he feels. Stop analyzing his behavior. Just *be*. That's it. Focus more on what you want and if he is a good match for you.

Ideally you should be so happy with yourself and so confident that you will get the relationship you want and deserve that you won't settle for anything that falls short. If you're not there yet, then ignore a few calls, cancel a few dates, and follow the "rules" until you're in a place where all of this comes naturally to you.

A funny thing about "games" is that they can help you improve your confidence by finally putting you in a position of power in your relationship. When you're more confident, it will show in the decisions you make and the way you carry yourself. This will lead to even more confidence and better decision-making.

It's not about the actions, it's the mindset. If the actions help you get into the right mindset, then great. But the actions alone won't really do anything because you can't keep up the charade for long, your true self will always come out eventually.

When The Chase Ends

I get a lot of panicked messages that go along the lines of: "Everything was going great but now he doesn't seem as interested. What do I do? How do I get him to chase me again?!"

It's an inevitable part of a relationship and how you handle it has more to do with you than him.

A woman who is confident and high value will not be alarmed when a man is no longer chasing her because she knows she is worthy of love and she is lovable. She doesn't see this pullback as meaning anything about her because she doesn't base her self worth on how he treats her and responds to her

A woman with weak self-esteem will start to spiral when a guy isn't chasing anymore. She'll obsess over it, she'll worry about it, she'll try to fix it, and as a result the dynamic is totally off.

So why will a man stop chasing? Basically, the chase has to end at some point. The "chase" or the pursuit is an important component to courtship but it's means to an end. Eventually it has to lead to something with a little more substance. And then there isn't as much of a need to chase at that level.

Also, a man will only chase you in proportion to how out of reach you are.

If he's caught you, if you're there, if you've been won, if you have given yourself to him fully, then there really isn't much of a need to chase.

In the beginning, his competitive drive is activated, he's trying to win you over. And the way he behaves isn't always an indicator of how much he likes you because he doesn't really know you yet. In the beginning he's really trying to get you to like him—and yes of course he also has a baseline level of interest in you but he can't really like you until he knows you.

Here is how to respond when he's not chasing or pursuing you with as much fervor:

1. Relax

When a man stops chasing, you have to *relax*. You have to be calm about it. No good comes from being in a panicked, frenzied state of mind.

When the panicked thoughts creep in...is he losing interest?...Did I do something wrong?...Am I losing him?...Why does nothing ever work out for me?...I'm going to end up alone...

I want you to stop and notice the thought and then ask: *Does this thought serve me well? Does it take me where I want to go?* And the answer is no! It doesn't serve you, it activates your fears and insecurities so stop engaging with the thought and shift your focus onto something more positive and productive.

2. Don't Try To Win Him Over

Chasing him is *not* the way to get him to chase you. Get back into a prize mentality and remember a prize does not plot and strategize ways to get a guy.

3. Give Him The Space To Pursue You

You can show interest, that's not a bad thing. You can make the first move, you can initiate plans, but you can't do *all* the work. It's too aggressive and too desperate and doesn't give him any space to invest in you. And that is a prerequisite for him to develop feelings for you.

So don't always text first, don't always initiate the plans, don't fill every silence with something creative and interesting to say, he can put in some effort as well!

4. Watch Your Energy

Stop obsessing and being desperate to hear from him, that is an energy of lacking, that is a needy energy. You need to instead be in a place of knowing that everything is OK, everything is as it should be. I will get the love I want. That is very different than desperately hoping and wishing he reciprocates your feelings.

And above all, instead of focusing on why he's not chasing you... ask yourself: *Why do I care? What wants/needs/fears am I attaching onto this person?*

A lot of the time when we feel that obsessive pull toward something it's coming from an unhealthy place. This person has come to represent something to us and about us. Be honest and look within to see what it is.

The Truth About "Good" Relationships

A lot of us have grand ideas about what a "good relationship" with the "right person" looks like. If you're single, you use this vision as fuel to keep you going through the lonely nights and bad dates, telling yourself that one day all the pain will be worth it. You believe there is a light at the end of the tunnel, a man who will be everything you've ever wanted and make you happier than you ever thought possible. If you're in a relationship, you question if you should stay when things get rocky or problems arise. These doubts make you wonder if he really is the man for you, because aren't you supposed to "just know" when the right one comes along? And if that is the case, then are these moments of uncertainty a sign that it's not right?

It's no secret that our society idealizes love. Starting in early childhood we get inundated with idealized portrayals of eternal love, from Disney movies to Nicholas Sparks novels. We develop expectations of what love should be, how it should feel, what it should look like...and we feel disappointed when reality doesn't quite align with those expectations.

Here's the thing that no one really tells you: good relationships don't always *feel* all that good, but it's not for the same reason bad relationships feel bad.

Bad relationships are the ones filled with drama. The highs are higher and the lows are lower. When I say "bad relationship," I mean everything from a toxic, codependent situation to a relationship with a man who won't commit in a significant way, to a match that is simply incompatible.

These "bad relationships" are a great escape from real life. They give you the chance to lose yourself in someone else's drama...or escape from your own. When you're spending hours trying to figure out how he feels, where this is going, what he meant when he said x, why he's taking so long to text back; you don't really have to face yourself. You lose yourself in the emotional high of it all. It's even better if you're dealing with a guy who comes with a lot of emotional baggage. Investing in his problems is like a vacation from dealing with your own.

But in a good relationship—a relationship where you're on the same page, where you aren't waiting anxiously for the next text, where you aren't wondering if he likes you because you know exactly how he feels—well, those are the relationships that bring you face to face with who you truly are. Sometimes they bring out the best in you, because we all have inherent goodness within us. And sometimes they bring out the worst in you, because a lot of us have been burned or are holding on to traumas from the past that we didn't even realize were still buried within us.

Sometimes there will be nothing wrong in the relationship, but you'll feel sad or anxious or upset. You won't be able to blame this on the fact that he didn't call or text, or that you're not his girlfriend or he hasn't said "I love you," because he never leaves you hanging, he is proud to call you his girlfriend, he adores you, and you know it. These feelings aren't coming from him; they're coming from you. If you've been hurt in the past, this feeling of unease comes from your own deep-seated trust issues. If regardless of his behavior you can't seem to trust that he'll be there for you, then this is your own fear of abandonment rising to the surface, and it's something you need to face yourself.

In a good relationship, your actions, your mindset, your behavior, the things you say, they all impact someone else. Sometimes you'll really hurt your partner and realize how insensitive you can be. Sometimes he'll say something innocent and it will cause a huge fight because that innocent comment hit an open wound of yours you didn't even know existed.

Sometimes you'll feel unloved, insecure, angry. Sometimes you'll want to just run, and sometimes you'll feel really lonely, and that will surprise you, because how can you be lonely in the company of someone who truly loves you?

Some will make the mistake of thinking this is the wrong relationship, and they'll leave. Some will blame their partner for "making" them feel a certain way, and issues will continue to arise until the relationship implodes. Others will realize that you can't let love in from the outside if you don't feel it on the inside and will do the hard inner work to get there. They will face their demons and deal with the pain from the past. They will communicate openly and honestly with their partners about their fears and their doubts, and they won't hold on to anger and resentment. They will realize that all relationships, even the best ones, take work, but it starts with working on yourself.

There's this idea that in the right relationship, everything will just be perfect. He'll be the other half of your soul, you'll reach a level of happiness you never knew existed, you'll feel secure and comfortable and confident. A good relationship can give you these things for sure, but not on its own. It has to start from within. If you don't already feel good, if you still have issues to work through, if you have a void within, you will never fully be able to trust him, and you will never truly feel "good enough." No matter how many sweet things he says or does, you will never be able to give and receive love freely.

When we're single, we're often unaware of the work that needs to be done because those parts of us that are hurt and need to be healed don't get accessed. Or maybe we do know but think the right guy will make it all better. Love forces you to face yourself. It brings up all the unloved parts. And you can't hide who you are when you are in a good, loving relationship. Instead, you are forced to face it and deal with it. Your partner will always reflect back who you really are (and vice versa). And everything that happens will be much more emotionally significant.

When all you've had are bad relationships, it's hard to really know what you're doing when a good one comes along. You're not used to this feeling of things just being right. You're not used to just coasting along on placid waters and you can't trust it. Instead, you stand on high alert, waiting for a storm to roll in and knock you overboard. For some of us, it might genuinely feel weird to just know how a guy feels about us and not have to guess and decode and look for clues. It can be unfamiliar, and we may take it to mean something is amiss and worry we're overlooking something. Maybe we pick him apart, maybe we start fights, maybe we feel despair because this isn't how it's supposed to be.

Someone may be perfect for you, but they still won't be a perfect person. And you're not a perfect person. And the relationship won't be perfect, but it will force each of you to deal with your issues and work on yourselves to be better. In the right relationship, you want to be your best self—not just for your sake, but because you're accountable to him and you don't want to cause him any hurt and pain. But the path to becoming your best self isn't always a smooth one. There are bumps and sharp turns and it can be dark and scary sometimes, but it's OK. In fact, it's normal.

The road to becoming our best selves takes time, patience, and a lot of work. It involves gaining an awareness of what we need to work on and finding the tools to get there.

Here are a few key things you can do to make a "good" relationship even better:

1. Manage Your Thoughts

Emotionally generated thoughts tend to become magnified and then multiply. Let's say one day your wonderful, loving partner doesn't text you back for hours. In the moment maybe you start to get upset and think, "I can't believe he didn't answer that sweet text I just sent him; I know he always has his phone on him and is constantly checking it. He must not care about me, or maybe he's having doubts. He never shows me he cares (then insert a running tab of all the instances, big or small, where you didn't feel cared for by him). I can't believe I'm with a guy who doesn't appreciate me, I don't deserve this," and on and on.

The more the thoughts come flooding in, the more upset you'll become. Instead of continuing down this road, cut the flow of thoughts off at the source. Shift your thinking: *OK, he didn't text me back right away so it must mean he's in a meeting or got tied up. He cares about me, I know he does. He texts back right away the majority of the time. His feelings didn't suddenly change; that just wouldn't make any logical sense.*

Try to identify your faulty line of thinking and gain a more objective awareness. Look for the good in him and the good in your relationship and focus on that instead of participating in a negative line of thinking that isn't serving you in any positive way. Remember, when thoughts flood in, notice them, look at each one, and ask: *Does this serve me well?*

2. Tell Him What You're Feeling

I mentioned earlier that sometimes we can suddenly feel hurt or upset by something minor. When this happens, it usually isn't the result of what's going on in the present, it's because some hurt from the past was triggered. If you find yourself feeling scared or upset, just be open and tell him.

Being vulnerable is what strengthens emotional bonds. In a healthy, loving relationship we need to trust that we can be vulnerable with our partners without them using our disclosures against us. If something happens and you feel an emotional response, tell him what's going on. Maybe you say something like, "I really care about you and I want to get closer to you, but I've been hurt badly in the past and sometimes my fear of being hurt again gets triggered."

These honest disclosures will not scare him away; if anything, they'll make him feel even closer to you and make him want to protect you from feeling these negative emotions even more. When you get angry or defensive or blame him for making you feel a certain way, then you activate his fears and his defenses and it pushes him away.

No matter what darkness you have inside, being open and honest about it and sharing it in a loving way will strengthen your bond. As long as it's done without blame or shame, you can basically tell him anything.

3. Manage Your Mood

The only person you can control is yourself. You can inspire a man to feel and do certain things, but you can never force it out of him. A lot of us fall into the role of being victims of circumstance. We let the things that happen dictate how we feel when really that's our decision to make. Yes, sometimes something will happen and you'll have an immediate emotional response, but it's up to you to decide if that incident ruins your day or not. Ultimately your mood is largely under your control.

When you bring a happy, positive mood into your interactions with your guy, it's contagious. When he experiences that positive energy, he feels happy and empowered and he wants to do more and give more and be even better in the relationship. It is only when a man feels defeated or feels like a loser who can't make his woman happy that he retreats and doesn't engage in those loving behaviors.

4. Resolve Your Issues, Don't Wait For Them To Resolve Themselves

A good relationship will always bring your unresolved issues to the surface. That's because good relationships with partners who love us force us to be at our best...and in order to be our best, we have to deal with and rid ourselves of our worst. Whether it's insecurity, poor self-esteem, fear of abandonment, or character flaws like being insensitive, impatient, or selfish...they all come out. You can try to shove them to the side, but they'll keep coming back until they are properly dealt with.

Love can be healing in some ways, but your partner is not responsible for your emotional well-being, only you are. The path to resolution will be different for everyone. Some will find the answers on their own, some may find it in a self-help book, and some will want to work with a therapist.

The worst thing you can do is nothing. Problems don't just work themselves out on their own; you won't wake up one day and discover that all your issues are gone. Time doesn't heal all wounds, that's a myth. You have to do the work with time, otherwise you'll stay stuck indefinitely and those wounds will follow you around like gum stuck to the bottom of your shoe.

The greatest service you can do for yourself and your relationship is to be growth oriented and always strive to be your best self.

5. Tell Him What You Want

Even the best boyfriend or husband in the world isn't going to give you exactly what you want all the time because he doesn't always know what that is, so the best way to get it is to just tell him! Men are not responsive to nagging or criticism, but they can be enormously receptive—and appreciative—when you tell them what makes you happy in a loving way.

This feels *so* much better than being upset at him for not doing something and holding it in and silently resenting him for it. When you do that, you transmit a punishing vibe that hangs in the air and poisons everything, making him even less likely to do what you want.

We all give and experience love in different ways. Even in the best relationship, you aren't going to feel completely loved all the time. Again, some of this is the result of your own stuff and some of it is because he doesn't always know what to do to make you feel loved. When you tell him, then you free yourself from the confines of feeling resentful and unloved and he feels better because now he can rise up and be the amazing man you need and deserve. So everyone wins.

How To Stop Stressing Over Your Relationships

One of the biggest relationship mistakes I see women make is stressing over their relationship, whether it's in the dating stage or in a more established relationship.

The stressing is tied to a fear of losing the guy, and what that will mean to her. It almost feels like a way to protect ourselves from getting hurt but it doesn't have the intended effect and instead we may set the stage for the exact scenario we fear to come to life.

When you stop stressing out over the relationship, you are free to really be *in* the relationship. You can see the other person for who he is, and you can give yourself to him freely–no strategies, no game-playing, no manipulation. You won't feel a need to control anything. You can just *be*, and there is no greater feeling than that.

But how do we do it? How do we stop our minds from spinning into overdrive, sending out waves of unpleasant thoughts and sounding alarm bells?

1. Realize Stressing Gets You Nowhere

First, you need to realize that getting all wound up over the state of your relationship serves no purpose, ever. It causes problems within the relationship but more importantly, it takes a huge toll on your sense of self and self-esteem. When you care too much, you inevitably become attached to a certain outcome. You invest mental energy in making sure things go a certain way. And if they don't, then you suffer on many levels.

I have been guilty of stressing over past relationships. It was always the same pattern. Things started out fun and light, I got excited about the possibilities...and then became scared that my imagined future wouldn't come to be...and then panic set in. From then on, the relationship was no longer enjoyable. Every interaction and conversation became a test to see exactly where he stood and how he felt.

Anyone who has dated long enough knows exactly what I'm talking about. The problem is that our minds trick us into believing there is some sort of payoff to this type of thinking. Like it will somehow lead us to a place of confidence and clarity. It won't. It will lead you in the opposite direction and cause you to feel even more uncertain and insecure.

2. See A Relationship For What It Is

Let's talk about what a relationship is and isn't. We'll start with what it isn't. A relationship isn't a measure of your worth or worthiness in this world. It is not there to serve you and give you things like happiness and self-esteem. It is not there to make you feel good about life and about yourself. This isn't to say a relationship *can't* do these things, it's just that these aren't the elements upon which a healthy relationship is built.

A relationship also isn't some sort of milestone, a sign that you've "made it," that you will be OK, that you are now a member of some elite club. It isn't something you work to acquire. It is not a goal to achieve.

A relationship is an experience to be had and shared. It is about discovering how compatible you are with someone else, and if there is enough chemistry and compatibility to form a lifelong partnership. The only work you have to do is to make sure you are your best self and get to a place where you can give and receive love. No amount of plotting or analyzing will change whether you and someone else are compatible. You either are or you aren't. The dating process is more of a discovery process to find out if it's there.

So you enter into the relationship as your best self and then one of two things happens: it works out, or it doesn't. And if it doesn't, you're OK because you know that it just means you weren't a match with that person. It doesn't mean you're flawed or damaged or bad or unlovable. It just wasn't a match. Sometimes you'll be able to see this, and sometimes the other person will have that clarity. Either way, if it doesn't work, it's because it wasn't the right fit. That's all!

If you can realize this, *really* realize it, then there will be absolutely nothing to stress over.

3. Set A Freak-Out Deadline

A lot of us make the mistake of prematurely freaking out over something that really turns out to be absolutely nothing. For example, let's say you start seeing a new guy and things are going great. You talk regularly, go on fun dates, it seems to be going really well. But then you don't hear from him for a day or two and immediately hit the panic button.

And then the devastation starts to creep in, followed by the doubts. *What did I do wrong? Was it something I said? Something I did? Why do the guys I like always leave me?* You feel a sense of dread deep in your gut and you know, you just *know*, that he's never coming back.

Meanwhile, in boy land, he's been really slammed at work and has barely had a minute to come up for air. In his mind, the relationship is going great, he's happy to have met a great girl like you and he can't wait to finish this big project so he can see you again. He's happily going along doing his thing while you are knee-deep in heartbreak mode, mourning the loss of what could have been and trying to figure out where it all went wrong.

And just when the agony is at its peak, he calls! And everything is fine! You're relieved, but at the same time, you are so *in it* now. You cling to the relationship even tighter because you remember how miserable it felt when you thought you'd lost it, and you vow not to do anything to screw this up.

I'm not saying the relationship will be doomed after this point, but I can guarantee it will cause a major shift in the dynamic and it will definitely ruin your ability to actually enjoy the relationship anymore.

Rather than reflexively panicking when something seems amiss, set a deadline. For example, if you started seeing a guy and don't hear from him for a day or two, say, "I will not panic about this right now. If I don't hear from him by this day at this time, then I am allowed to be upset," and then just take it out of your mind.

This also works if you're in a more established relationship. Let's say you don't see your partner as often as you'd like. Maybe you'd like to go on dates more regularly or see him a few times during the week. Tell yourself that you will be fine with things for the time being, and if nothing changes in two weeks, then you can be upset about it and deal with it. Or let's say you're in a serious relationship and there has been talk of getting engaged, but he hasn't popped the question yet. Instead of getting angry about it, just give yourself a deadline. If he doesn't propose in the next month, then I will be upset and I will deal with it. Until then, I'm going to enjoy the relationship and not let this bother me.

This little exercise will help you train your mind to stay calm and avoid spinning into a frenzy. It will help you gain control over your thoughts and your mood, and this will be of major benefit to you and your relationship. And the funny thing is, whatever problem you wanted to get really upset about right away usually resolves itself before the deadline you set! I'm telling you, it really works.

4. Be Present

The biggest problem with stressing over your relationship is that it takes you out of the relationship and into a place that's not real. When you get stressed and anxious, you're no longer interacting with the person sitting in front of you, you're interacting with the thoughts in your mind. You fixate on an imagined future and worry about how and if you'll get there with him. Stop doing this!

Instead, just be present. Be right here, right now. When you go on a date with a guy, whether it's the first or the fiftieth, all you should be thinking about is enjoying your time with him and building a connection. If you're in the early stages of dating, the only thing to decide is whether you want to go on another date with this person (and save that consideration for after the date). Don't size him up and look for signs that he's the one and this is *it*. Don't scan him to determine how he feels and if he likes you. Just enjoy it for what it is and let the process unfold organically. *No stress!*

When you worry about where this is going and if there's a future, you blind yourself to what's in front of you and hinder your chances of forming a real connection. You can't connect with someone who isn't there with you in that present moment. Most people don't see other people, they only see their concerns of the moment, and they clutter their minds trying to figure out how he feels, what he's thinking, and so forth. The concern and worry and doubt feels like it's serving a purpose, but it's not! It's actually taking you further away from where you want to be. A relationship is what's in front of you, that's it!

Now I'm not saying you should never think about the future or discuss where things are heading, there is a time for that. Discussing the relationship or the future isn't the problem, the problem occurs when the *mindset* you have about the relationship revolves around what you want and are afraid you won't get, instead of what you have. When you're full of anxiety and fear, and you panic thinking about what will or won't be in the future, you have an unhealthy mindset. The best way to fix this is to try to just be present.

5. Stop Fixating On What Things Supposedly Mean

As women, we've all been programmed to see having a relationship as some sign that we've made it, that we're worthy. Being single is seen as something to be pitied and being in a relationship is something to covet. As a result, a lot of us measure our worth by our relationship status. If a guy leaves, that means we're unworthy and we weren't good enough to have this thing that we've been told we need in order to be good enough. It's hard to undo years of faulty programming when it's been so firmly ingrained into our psyche, but it is possible.

Remember, only you can determine your own worth. You won't get a sense of your own value from a bottle or from a man or by splurging on the latest trends. *You* set the standard for how valuable you are. You do this by living a rich, fulfilling life filled with things you love. You do things that make you happy, you work on improving yourself, you develop your talents, you take care of yourself, you do things that tap into your essence and allow you to express your true self. *This* is how self-esteem is built. If you wrap up your identity in what men think of you, or what your relationship status is, you will never ever feel satisfied.

In any relationship, you need to have faith in yourself and trust that no matter what happens, you will be OK and you can handle whatever life throws at you. Anytime you start to panic, anytime your mind starts spinning and you worry that he'll leave, that he's losing interest, that he's not that into you and *what are you going to do if he leaves? How will you go on?* Remember: you'll be fine! You were fine before you met him and you'll be fine if he decides to leave. You are OK. Everything will be OK. Say it to yourself as many times as you need to, until it really penetrates!

How To Play The Relationship Game Without Getting Crushed

A little while back I met up with some girlfriends to catch up. I love meeting up with my single girlfriends because: A) As a mom, I don't get as much adult interaction as I crave! And B) I get a lot of new material, let's be honest!

Basically, one of my friends met a guy and they hit it off. The catch is that he lives in a different country. After they parted ways they continued to stay in touch and had regular Skype dates. Eventually, they planned a weekend where they would meet up in person. Everything went great, their connection was strong, but on the flight home my friend started to panic.

She was terrified that things were going too well and what if something went wrong? What if he stopped liking her? What if the distance became too much? What if he started pulling away?

And he didn't even mention when they would see each other again, that's a bad sign! Oh no, it must mean he doesn't want to see her again, that he isn't serious, that she's going to get hurt. And if she gets hurt again, then what will she do?

This is basically what flooded her mind for the entire six-hour flight.

Now onto another friend. She met a guy online a while back and two weeks later they were boyfriend/girlfriend. I was concerned about the pace of the relationship, but she seemed happy so I let it be. And she was so happy.

He was everything she has ever wanted and she really thought this was it. Now you can imagine her utter shock when after four months of dating bliss he showed up one day and dumped her. It seemed they were in two completely different relationships. In hers, she was happy and everything was great and she had never been treated so well by a guy. In his, he was unhappy and felt unappreciated and resented her for various things. She had no idea he was feeling any of this, and she is not an oblivious person!

She was absolutely beyond repair distraught for many months.

But time marched on and she started to bounce back, but not really. She was still thinking about her ex and couldn't let it go. Then suddenly he was back in the picture.

They started seeing each other again but weren't "official." This went on for several months and she was really frustrated. It was especially surprising given how quick he was to call her his girlfriend the first time around. Then one day our other good friend came across him on a dating app and my friend totally freaked. It was clear that he wasn't in it, that he wasn't serious, that she was the only one investing, and that he had some major issues to deal with.

The red flags were there all along, and if it wasn't apparent to her, I pointed them all out after the first time they broke up! I saw right through her ex from the beginning. It's not that I didn't think he was a good guy, but he was a mess, or a damage case as I call it. He had way too many issues and until he solved them, he wouldn't be able to be in a relationship.

She knew all this, but she still went back, and she got hurt all over again.

When we were having our catch up, she expressed frustration with herself for not being over it by now (this was a few months after their second breakup). Why was it still bothering her? Why couldn't she let it go? Why does she still think about him?

It was pretty obvious to me what the problem was in both of these scenarios, even though the situations are vastly different. It's something I write about a lot.

Both girls attached way too much to the outcome. They invested in fantasy futures and put too much weight in their investment.

Now it was perfectly clear in my mind, but when I said this to them they were both a little confused. What do you mean? How can you not invest?

Let's break it down further.

For the first friend, my advice was simple: she needed to gain control over her thoughts. She needed to say to herself: *I am fine, everything is OK. I was OK before I met this guy and I'll be fine if things don't work out.* This is my go-to mantra and it never fails.

What she was doing is the opposite. She was getting overly invested in a relationship that didn't even exist just yet. She was making herself feel like the world was going to end if she didn't hear from him again, or if things didn't work out. Notice I say making herself feel. This was entirely her doing, he did nothing to create such panic and fear within her. When she heard me say this, she eased up a lot. "Wow, you're right. I'll be FINE!"

Onto the next. So this is something I've done and many of you have done.

You meet a great guy—finally—and you get really excited. And it's not like you're delusional, he's really into you too! Everything is great! You're official, you meet the parents, you share your deep thoughts and feelings, it's all great. But then it all goes wildly off track. It happens so fast you don't even realize what just happened. You try to ignore the red flags because you need this to work. You don't want to start all over again, to go back out there and sift through all the losers to find that one gem who might have potential. You already found him and you won't let this go!

But sometimes you don't have a choice. He lets go and you can't do anything about it.

What you need to do, especially in an early relationship when you don't really know the other person, is mentally keep your options open. I did this with my husband because I had been hurt so many times before and I didn't want to mess this up. After our first date, it was clear this was something. But I wasn't going to allow myself to be swept away into fantasy land.

Instead, I told myself that yes, I was excited and wow, we have such a strong connection, and *woah*, I can't believe our date was almost eight hours long...and it would be great if this works out, it would be so romantic especially since we dated in high-school and he was my first love...but if it doesn't work out *I WILL BE FINE.*

Before we went out on our first date I was casually talking to two other guys who were interested in dating me.

One of them lived in another state and we had been trying to work out the logistics, the other had been traveling a lot and was finally getting settled back in. Before I could go out with either of them I went on a date with my husband.

While I wanted to call it off with the other two, I didn't. Even though I didn't think either was right for me, I let myself envision a possible future with both. I didn't attach to any particular outcome. Either I would end up with my high school sweetheart, and aw how sweet that would be?! Or I would end up with the guy who lives down south, and that would be cool! Or maybe I would end up with bachelor number 3 who lives a few blocks away from me and also traveled to Italy over the summer and was there at the exact same time as me and what a crazy coincidence?! Or I'll end up single for longer and that's not so bad! I honestly loved being single, I had a blast and would have been fine staying that way.

I knew no matter what, I would be OK. Everything would be OK. I didn't get so caught up in possible future scenarios, I entertained the various ways things could go down, and I was happy with all the possible outcomes. And because I wasn't worried about the future, I could enjoy the present. My husband made it "official" pretty early on and it was at that point that I dropped the other suitors. I didn't actually go out with them, but we were still texting and talking and I still kept the door open, until it was time to shut it.

Once we were in an official relationship, I made an effort to just enjoy it and not freak myself out over the prospect of things not working out. I decided not to solve any problems until there were problems to solve and fortunately, things worked out pretty nicely.

So that's how it's done. That's what I mean when I say don't attach to the outcome, don't engage in a fantasy future, just be present. That's how to enjoy dating and relationships without becoming jaded or desperate or a battered shell of your former self.

Remember this: Stop freaking out! Relationships aren't that hard, they only feel hard because we stress over them for no reason and create problems when there aren't any. Everything will be OK, just relax and trust the timing of your life.

CHAPTER 8

What Guys Want in a Woman & from a Relationship

"The greatest happiness of life is the conviction that we are loved; loved for ourselves, or rather, loved in spite of ourselves." —Victor Hugo

As I've said many times over, the most essential ingredient to having an amazing relationship is to love yourself and love your life. When you can check those things off the list, then everything else falls into place. Again, I'm not saying if it's not working out it's all your fault and all on you. A relationship is a partnership, it's about working together and creating a deep and meaningful connection. It's not about one person bending over backward to make the other happy or trying to be whatever he needs.

I've spent a lot of time talking about you, so now let's talk about *him*, specifically what he wants and needs from a relationship. Personally, I loved discovering this stuff. It made the male gender a slightly less foreign entity to me and made relationships so much more fun and enjoyable.

I no longer had to bang my head against the wall trying to figure him out, I just got it. I knew what he was thinking and why he was being a certain way. I also knew what to do in order to get my needs met in the relationship. This is true of when I was single and dating around and still holds true now that I'm married. Knowledge is a powerful thing; use it wisely!

The Main Difference Between Men & Women In Relationships

There are many differences between men and women, both in the way we're designed physically and the way we process things emotionally. And I'm sure you've noticed that the way we view relationships is also very different. The main problem in a lot of relationships is that women don't know what men want.

While the differences may seem vast, they're pretty simple when you break it down. Once you can understand the differences, you'll have a much easier time understanding your guy and making your relationship even more amazing.

I want to preface this by saying that I know there are exceptions. To be clear, I'm going to be speaking about the way men and women are *in general.*

In general, the appeal of a relationship for women is *the relationship*. Women naturally gravitate towards the idea of marriage and see it as highly appealing. An ideal relationship for a woman is one where she feels understood and connected to her significant other. An ideal man is one who truly *understands* her and cares for her.

The ideal relationship for a man is one where he gets to feel like *the man*. Men like to feel acknowledged, respected, and appreciated. Men often enjoy the role of being givers, so for a man, the ideal woman may be one who can happily receive. There is nothing sexier or more appealing to him than a happy woman who appreciates everything he has to offer, not just physically, but also emotionally, spiritually, and intellectually.

While men love to give, they don't always know what you need and most relationship problems arise from basic communication malfunctions where a woman goes about trying to tell a man what she needs in the wrong way.

For instance, if your partner is hardly ever home, rather than saying: "Why aren't you ever home?" say, "I really love it when you're here." If your partner isn't meeting your needs, it is always a much better strategy to tell him what you *do* want rather than constantly hammering in what you don't want and pointing out the ways in which he's failing to meet your needs.

Remember, he *wants* to make you happy, and the more appreciated he feels the more he will go out of his way to give you what you want.

It's also worth noting that men respond to specific compliments much better than abstract ones. For instance, saying something like: "Thank you for doing the dishes, that was so thoughtful of you," packs more of a punch than something general like "You're so thoughtful." This can be an area of confusion since women are thrilled with general compliments (you're so smart/pretty/nice/funny/etc.)

While the principles I've outlined may seem fairly straightforward and universally understood, they often get completely ignored. The biggest mistake most women make in relationships is assuming men think just like they do.

The key to a successful relationship is communicating your needs in a way that the other person can *hear*. If you attack or blame, your guy will completely shut down and tune you out. If you come from a place of compassion and appreciation, he will tune in to exactly what you're saying and will try to do whatever he can to make you happy.

It's only when we embrace our differences and see the other side more clearly that healthy communication can flourish. Try it out and you'll see what I mean!

How To Be An Amazing Partner

There is so much misinformation out there about what it takes to be a great partner. It's not about cooking his favorite food or wearing sexy lingerie or mastering some crazy sexual trick. (I'm not saying these things don't help, but they don't get to the heart of the matter!) Understanding how men think and what they need in a relationship makes an enormous difference in the way you're able to relate to one another.

The top prerequisite for being in a great relationship is to be your best self. A trap that many people in relationships fall into is blaming their partner when problems arise. Rather than seeing what they can do to make things better, they blame him for not being what they want and think that if only he did XYZ, *then* everything would be fine.

It doesn't work that way. You can't ever make someone what you want them to be. All you can do is bring your best. When you do this, the other person will usually rise up and match you at your level.

While every guy has his own preferences when it comes to the physical, there are several fundamental qualities that all men crave in a woman.

Here are the most essential ways to be the most amazing partner ever:

Be Direct (Not Passive-Aggressive)

The majority of problems in a relationship occur because the woman expects a man to meet her needs and then resents him when he doesn't. She doesn't ask for what she wants because he should just "know." She may drop hints to help him out and then become even more annoyed when he doesn't pick up on them. The man, in turn, gets frustrated that nothing he does seems to be good enough. Eventually he gets discouraged and stops trying, and she feels even more resentful. Neither side has bad intentions; the problem is they aren't communicating properly because men and women have very different styles of communication. Men do not pick up on nuances and subtleties in the same way women do; they need things spelled out in a clear and direct manner.

If you're mad at him, don't act passive-aggressive until he asks what's wrong (to which you may reply "nothing," which he'll take to mean nothing is wrong, after which you'll continue to simmer because he should freakin' know it's *something*!). Just tell him what he did wrong. In relationships it's not usually what you say, it's *how* you say it. If you tell a guy something he is doing is upsetting or hurting you, and you say it in a loving, compassionate way, I guarantee he will try to fix it. If you come from a place of anger or resentment, he'll shut down and will be less motivated to correct it. Sigmund Freud is regarded as one of the most brilliant minds in psychology and even he had no idea what women want, so how do you expect the average guy to know?

Most arguments in relationships stem from deeper underlying issues that never get discussed or resolved. Maybe a woman feels like her guy doesn't really care about her, or isn't committed to her because he isn't as attentive as he was in the beginning of the relationship. Instead of being direct about it, she freaks out on him if he doesn't call her back one night or doesn't do the dishes after she slaved away cooking dinner for him. From there a big fight may ensue over something trivial while the real issue goes untouched. When you want something, or don't want something, just *tell him*.

Appreciate Him

Most women don't realize how *starved* men are for appreciation; I certainly had no idea until I started writing about relationships full-time. The problem is that we usually love others the way we like to be loved, and women typically feel loved when a man is being giving and attentive to her and her needs. Because of that, many women will be extra giving to their man. While this is very nice and appreciated, it's not what men really crave.

What a man deeply desires is feeling acknowledged and appreciated for what he provides. He wants to feel like his efforts were a success. This applies to everything he does from taking you out to a fancy dinner to taking out the trash.

If he takes you out on a nice date, acknowledge and appreciate him for it and tell him you had an amazing time. Men are typically more responsive to compliments about something they've done rather than who they are.

When a woman really sees and appreciates her man, it makes him feel like the ultimate winner and makes him want to do anything to keep her happy.

Remember back in chapter four I told you about that guy I really liked who said he didn't want to date me because he didn't want to ruin the friendship and then he dated my friend with no fear? First, seeing that all unfold was awful and my self-esteem took a major hit but in hindsight I realized he and I would never have worked out and we did end up becoming really close friends. She and him also didn't work out. He dumped her out of the blue and she was devastated and he didn't really give her a clear reason why. But he told me the reason. He said it was because she was too entitled and he felt like she didn't appreciate anything he did, she just expected it of him.

Now knowing her, I think she thought she was presenting herself as a high-value woman and I know she felt very intimidated dating him (he was gorgeous...successful...nice...charming, he was almost too good to be true). But it backfired. By expecting him to do all these things for her, she just turned him off and he was totally over it after about two months.

Another important relationship skill is to try to see the intention behind an action, and appreciate that. I have a personal example for this. Years ago I was dating a guy and one night he called and asked if he could come over. It was getting late and I was exhausted, but he said he'd be over in a half hour so I agreed. An hour and half later he still hadn't arrived and I was fuming! *Where could he be? Why is he even bothering to come over this late? Why do I have to wait up for him when I just need sleep!* He finally showed up carrying something that smelled delicious. I immediately went off on him for making me wait up for him and he sheepishly said, "I'm sorry, I wanted to surprise you and bring over a quesadilla from that place you love because I know you've been working so hard and barely have time to eat." Even though I was starving and had been *fiending* for a quesadilla, my anger had been building for an hour and didn't subside, and the rest of the night was uncomfortable and tense.

The mistake I made was in looking at the action (him being late), rather than the intention (him wanting to do something nice to make me happy). I'm not saying I shouldn't have been annoyed by his lateness, but the night probably would have gone a lot differently had I at least appreciated his good intentions...then later I could have nicely mentioned that the next time there was an hour-long line at the place, he should just buy me a bag of chips and call it a day!

No one is perfect and no matter how great your relationship, there will be times when he isn't doing something exactly the way you'd like him to. You'll get a lot further, and do a huge service to your relationship, if you focus on what he *is* doing right rather than focusing on what he isn't.

Give Him Space When He Needs It

Another major difference between men and women is in the way they handle stress and difficulties. While women typically seek out their friends and want to talk about it, men would rather retreat into the proverbial "man cave" and deal with it on their own. A woman might get upset when this happens and think he's shutting her out, but it really has nothing to do with her—it's just how he deals with things.

If your partner seems stressed out and begins to withdraw, just let him be. Don't coddle him or offer unsolicited advice or get on his case about why he isn't confiding in you. If he wants to talk about it with you, he will. If he doesn't and you continue to push him, you will just be another source of stress in his life that he needs to deal with, and he'll withdraw even further.

Men intuitively know that it isn't easy for women to give them space when they need it, so if you can do it without feeling angry or resentful, you'll be the woman who touches him more deeply than any other.

Maintain Your Own Life Outside Of The Relationship

Don't be that girl who completely falls off the map after she gets into a relationship.

Women make this mistake all the time (myself included!) They get into a relationship and the guy becomes the center of their universe. This is never healthy! For one thing, it kind of puts your relationship in a holding pattern and creates a scenario where you can be dating for years and years without taking the next step. If a guy is getting all of you, all the time, there's no reason for him to take that extra step...but that's a whole different discussion.

Another issue is that your relationship can't be your only source of happiness and fulfillment; you need to have a balanced life with several components filling you up in different areas. If you throw all of that away for your guy, then you add a lot of pressure to the relationship and will never feel completely satisfied with what you're getting from it (mostly because no one can be your everything). You may start to resent your partner and feel that he owes you more since you gave up so much for him, but that's not fair because the sacrifices you made were *your* choice. Another reason not maintaining your own life outside of the relationship is problematic is that you may end up staying in a bad relationship for far longer than you should because, well, you have nothing else to go back to.

Men typically fall in love with a woman in her absence, not her presence. If you're always there, he won't experience that deepening of the bond. To keep your relationship fresh and invigorating, it's essential to have time apart to do your own things. It gives you a break from the emotional intoxication of the relationship so you can see things more objectively, and it also takes some pressure off of the relationship and allows it to unfold more organically. I know it's tempting to hang out with him every time he asks, I know it's flattering when a guy wants so much of your time, I know you may think it's because he is just *so* crazy about you...and maybe he is, but giving in every single time is just not a good strategy. If he's a decent guy, he'll respect your boundaries and will encourage you to do your own thing on occasion.

Take Care Of Yourself

Don't stop working out, eating healthy, getting waxed, shaving your legs, blow-drying your hair, or any other healthy or beautifying activity that was a part of your life pre-relationship. Yes, it's easy to slide into a more *laissez-faire* approach when you're in a relationship, but if you do that then it won't be long before you're searching up and down to retrieve the burning spark that once existed.

Look, you don't need to be red carpet ready at all times, but you really should make an effort to try to maintain your appearance and look good for your guy. You put your best face forward during those first few months of dating, and there's no reason for it to stop once things are more established. It will keep the passion and lust alive in your relationship and also, it makes a man feel really good when a woman puts in effort to look beautiful for him.

The funny thing I notice is that women in relationships (again, myself included), will lounge around the house in sweats and a messy bun and no makeup when they're home with their guy, but will put on a face-full of makeup and get decked out when going out...to impress strangers? The whole thing is so backwards. While a man's love isn't solely contingent on physical appearance, it's really important (and attractive) to continue to take care of yourself like you did when you first met.

Be Positive

This is another tip that will enormously help your relationship, but also your life in general. Men cannot resist a woman with a smile. In fact, every guy I know has said that a positive attitude is the number-one most attractive quality a woman can have. Being happy all the time just isn't realistic. But a positive attitude is something that can get you through anything.

This kind of energy is infectious. It draws people towards you and it makes you the kind of woman a man will want to be with forever. Don't use your guy as a sounding board or your relationship as an emotional dumping ground. When your guy comes home, greet him with a smile...and then vent if you had a rough day and need to let it out.

Try to see the good in all situations, both in your relationship and outside of it. The things that happen in our lives, for the most part, are neutral. What makes them good or bad is our perceptions and the thoughts we attach to them.

There is really one thing every man wants in a woman: a woman who is easy to be around. That's pretty much it! That's the key to his heart. This doesn't mean you never have a complaint or a bad day. It means overall, it's just easy to be around you. It feels good. Again, this is something that will serve you well in your life overall, not just your relationships.

Respect Your Man

It goes without saying that an ideal woman is one who respects herself, but she also genuinely respects her man.

In addition to needing to be appreciated, men have an enormous need to feel respected. This is true of all humans, but usually this desire burns stronger in men. A man feels respected when a woman appreciates who he is and what he needs and gives him space to express himself without making demands on him and prioritizing herself over him.

Respect means accepting that he needs certain things, even if they are in opposition to what *you* want or need. For example, when men get stressed or feel unbalanced, they usually like to retreat into their "cave" to sort things out. They don't necessarily like talking through the problem and would rather work it out on their own and then come back into the relationship re-charged.

So let's say your guy is having a hard time and needs some time alone, but you really want him to be open and honest with you and to share his feelings. Respecting him entails putting what's best for him above what you want. In this case, it would be giving him the space to work through his issues even though you would prefer that he talk to you about it, because that's what's going to be most beneficial for him.

It also means respecting who he is, how he lives his life, and what his opinions are. Respect does not look like rolling your eyes when he says something you don't agree with (or think is the dumbest thing you've ever heard) and it doesn't look like not at least hearing him out and validating his opinion. It's never nice or fair to make someone feel like an idiot just because you don't quite see where they're coming from, and a really important skill is being able to listen to and respect another person's.

Respect Yourself

A man cannot love or care for a woman unless he respects her—it just won't happen. And a man cannot genuinely respect a woman who will put up with anything. While in theory a man would love to get away with everything, in reality there is nothing interesting or appealing about it. A lot of women are afraid to be firm in their convictions because they don't want to seem demanding or needy (which is funny because only needy people compromise on what they want).

Bending over backwards for a guy and letting him get away with treating you badly because you don't want to seem like a nag will guarantee more bad behavior, and eventually it will take a big hit on your sense of self. So figure out what you want and what you won't compromise on. And don't be afraid to walk away when he doesn't give you what you know you deserve. It's only when you're not afraid to walk away that he'll do anything to make you stay.

Putting up with poor treatment indicates you don't respect yourself. Each time you accept and forgive him for bad behavior, you are actually enforcing that it's OK for him to treat you badly.

At the core of having self-respect is having healthy boundaries. Having strong boundaries means you prioritize your needs and your emotions and do not assume responsibility for someone else's needs and emotions. When a woman has strong boundaries, she demonstrates confidence, self-respect, and a high sense of self-worth. Weak boundaries, on the other hand, are a sign of insecurity and low self-esteem.

If you don't have strong boundaries, a man doesn't have to work to get you. He can have you whenever he wants; you'll drop what you're doing to see him, you'll work around his schedule, his needs will suddenly become your needs. A guy might stick around for this, but this is not the kind of woman a man yearns for and deeply commits himself to.

A woman with healthy boundaries will not lose herself in a relationship and will not allow her identity to be entirely contingent upon how he sees her. She brings her best self to the relationship, and if problems arise she doesn't blame herself and assumes the responsibility for solving them. She acts in accordance with who she is and what she believes, and doesn't modify who she is for the sake of getting a guy or keeping him interested.

What Bad Boundaries Look Like

Heather was dating Ray for about a year, and their relationship was great aside from the fact that he wouldn't call her his girlfriend. The entire relationship was also operating according to his schedule. He had a stressful job and would work extremely long hours so she reasoned that it was only natural that they plan their time together around his schedule. If he had a night off, she would cancel whatever plans she had in order to see him. Sometimes he would disappear for days at a time with no explanation. If she called him out on it, he would get angry at her and remind her that they were not an official item and he could do as he pleased.

If she wanted to see him and he was busy, he would get annoyed. But if he wanted to see her, then he *had* to see her, and would call and text nonstop until she answered.

One night she was on a date with a new guy who had potential, but he was extremely turned off by the fact that her phone was blowing up the entire time. When she would confront Ray about how unreasonable it was for him to be able to do whatever he wanted, sometimes disappearing for days at a time, then get angry and upset when she wasn't available, he would turn everything around on her until she ended up apologizing to *him*. She finally got the strength to tell him that she could no longer continue seeing him if he didn't make a commitment, and even though he was upset, he let her go. Within a few weeks he was calling her again and asking to see her...and she would agree. (*I can't help it!* she'd exclaim. *I love him and want to see him.*) She was there for him whenever he needed her. Even at 4 am, if he wanted to see her, she would be there. But he was not always there when she needed him. Sometimes he would disappear and ignore her calls for weeks or even months. Then he would re-emerge and demand all her attention. And she always gave in.

After two years when Ray was in one of his disappearance modes she finally started to move on and began seeing someone new. Like clockwork, he re-emerged. After she ignored his calls for weeks, he showed up at her door, demanding to know why she'd been ignoring him. She told him she was seeing someone new, and he broke down and tearfully said he loved her. She felt bad for him and gave him another chance (by now, this would have been his 500th). He still wouldn't commit, still did whatever he wanted, still didn't respect her needs or her time, still was the exact same person. She attempted to cut it off many more times but it never stuck because she had no boundaries. Eventually he disappeared (I assume he found someone else to take advantage of) and she was left with endless, deeply rooted wounds to heal. Don't be like this!

Encourage Him To Meet Your Needs... Without Being Needy

While some of your previous relationships may have proven otherwise, the truth is. men are natural givers. Yes, that's right. They *want* to give, they want to provide, and they want to make you happy. What they don't want is to be bossed around and told what to do.

When a woman tells a man what to do, she is essentially emasculating him by taking away the very thing that makes him feel significant: his ability to provide. When you boss him around, he feels like a failure for not being able to do his job. Rather than wanting to do more for you, he feels defeated and retreats.

I'm not saying you should just let him do whatever he wants and not say a peep. There is a right way to encourage a guy to meet your fundamental needs (when I say needs, I mean universal needs we have as humans, like the desire to bond, connect, and support each other, not texting every hour on the hour), but it has to be done in a way that empowers him, not in a way that makes him feel like a failure. The fear of failure and desire to win is a driving force for most men in all areas of their life. Masculine energy is achievement oriented and fear failure more than anything else. Feminine energy most prioritizes relationships and primarily fears rejection and loss of love or connection

If you appreciate your man and are able to see him for who he is and love him for being that person, flaws and all, you are empowering him. When a woman is in a good place emotionally, she can empower her man effortlessly because it comes naturally to her. She brings out the best in him because she is coming from a place of love, not a place of control. She doesn't need him to validate her sense of self or be the one to heal her from her painful past. She is with him because she *wants* to be, not because she has some agenda.

Men want to feel manly and significant. They want to provide for you; it's just in their nature to be that way. However, a man will only want to give to a woman who can happily receive what he has to offer, not one who is going to make unnecessary demands in order to feel good about herself and secure in the relationship. A woman who tries to get this assurance from the outside will always be unsatisfied, and there is nothing more unappealing to a man than an unhappy woman.

Accept Him For Who He Is And Bring Out His Best

Often women get caught up in trying to turn a guy into what they want rather than accepting him as he is and encouraging him to become his best self.

Men can sense when women are trying to change or control them, and it isn't motivating—it's crippling and defeating. It makes men feel like failures and spurs them to do the opposite of what you wanted. In any relationship, it's imperative to accept other people for who they are, the good and the bad. The worst thing you can do is to try to turn him into what you need him to be. It may sound crazy, but women do this all the time!

Maybe you're trying to get him to be more emotionally supportive, more sensitive, more affectionate. I mean, all these things are great, but what you need to ask yourself is, are you trying to get him to be that way because it would be good for him or because it would be good for you?

An ideal woman accepts a man as he is, and since she is so accepting and appreciative he becomes a better man and a better partner, completely on his own. She brings her best self to the table and knows that by doing this, she will bring out his best self.

Be Confident And Secure In Yourself

This is perhaps the most essential imperative of all. In fact, if you can master this, doing everything else on this list will be easy and effortless.

There is nothing sexier or more appealing to a man than a woman who is thoroughly confident and truly loves her life.

Train yourself to see the good in who you are and what you have to offer. Learn to realize that any man would be beyond lucky to land you. See yourself as the ultimate prize. Even if you don't actually feel this way yet, say it to yourself anyway. Thoughts have a way of becoming reality, and eventually it will sink it.

The Number-One Thing Every Woman Needs To Know About Men

I constantly get asked to share the number one thing I've learned about men since I got into this business. I also wrote a book called "10 Things Every Woman Needs to Know About Men," and when it came out the only question I got asked was: "So what's the number-one thing I need to know?"

I used to have a few answers to this question, but in recent years it's become clear to me that there really is only one. There is one core thing to understand about men, and when you get it, everything else makes sense. It is the one thing that changed my relationship when I really realized what it means.

What it comes down to is how vital it is for a man to feel significant, like he's having a meaningful impact. You may have heard this before, but there is such a difference between hearing something and internalizing it.

Masculine energy is typically goal-oriented and focused. This is something we've all heard before, and most women know that men aren't as skilled at multitasking as we are. But let's go deeper and look at the reason.

The reason men are so focused and single-minded is because a man gains his sense of significance based on his ability to have an impact on the world. This doesn't mean relationships aren't important to men (they are), but in order for a man to feel good about himself and his life, he needs to feel significant, he needs to feel like he's winning. And when he feels like a winner, he can be the best man possible in a relationship. When he feels like a loser, he is at his absolute worst.

Even though I knew all about this concept, that didn't stop me from making my now husband feel like a loser when we were engaged and going through a rough patch. I couldn't quite help it. It was a stressful time and I felt like he was adding to my stress instead of helping me to alleviate it.

I know that I can be a direct, harsh, sometimes critical person. I see it as being a perfectionist, as striving for excellence. Sometimes this is a good thing, but other times it can be a very negative thing.

When I was engaged and dealing with all the stress that comes with planning a wedding, I moved on my own into our new apartment a few months before the big day and was greeted by something out of a horror movie: it was massively infested with roaches.

It was awful and disgusting and I was barely sleeping or eating, and I became angry and resentful because I didn't think he was being sympathetic or supportive enough based on what I had to deal with (his comment, "Relax, they're just bugs," really pushed me to a new level of seeing red).

I also felt like he was making wedding planning more stressful. He gave me a hard time about almost every aspect of the wedding, and I got mad at him for being so difficult and unsupportive. I was also mad that he wasn't as loving towards me as he used to be and that he now seemed uncomfortable around me. I was having a hard time and just needed him to be nice to me!

OK, long story short, we were both at fault in our own way. Both of us were being difficult and neither one of us was being empathetic to the other.

Things changed one day when, for once, we were discussing our issues lovingly and without blame and resentment, and he said to me, "I feel like I'm always failing you. Like I can never do anything right and everything I do is going to upset you or make you disappointed in me. That's why it's hard for me to be loving and comfortable around you."

It was a big slap-in-the-face moment. Here I was, this wise and worldly relationships expert, writing about how important it is to show a man appreciation and how important it is for a man to feel like a winner, and I was making the love of my life feel like a worthless loser.

I'm not saying he was totally innocent; he did do things that hurt me and he made a difficult time in my life even more difficult, but I still didn't handle it right.

I would get mad at him for expressing his feelings because it stressed me out, when really I should have listened to and acknowledged him. I didn't see the good intentions behind the ways he was trying to be there for me because I was so mad about all the things he was doing that I didn't like.

After we had that talk, I shifted gears and instead of making him feel bad about what he wasn't doing right, I lovingly showed my appreciation for what he *was* doing right. (This ties into a concept I've mentioned several times throughout this book: the only person you can change is yourself. I could have stayed mad and simmered in resentment because of what he did wrong, but where would that have gotten us?)

When a man feels like he's "winning" at making you happy, he goes out of his way to make you happy. After I changed my response to him, the entire relationship dynamic changed. He was so sweet and loving and *so* supportive and helpful in dealing with our unwanted houseguests. While at first the roaches put a strain on our relationship, once we started communicating properly and giving each other what the other needed (for him, feeling like a winner; for me, getting support and empathy), the whole ordeal ended up bringing us closer...seriously!

This is just one little example that illustrates a much larger point.

Resentment is poison for a relationship. Maybe you're mad at him and maybe it's justified, but harshly criticizing him or focusing on the negative will only make him feel like a loser. Once he feels like a loser, he'll start resenting you, which will in turn cause him to do things that make you resent him, and the cycle will continue. Someone needs to be the one to put a stop to it. While it isn't always easy, it is so worth it and will make such an incredible difference in your relationship. Being compassionate and loving is always the solution. Being negative and critical always causes more problems than it solves.

How Gratitude Changes Everything

One of the first life lessons little kids are taught is to always say, "Thank you." When people do something nice for you, you thank them. It's a concept that is drummed into our heads starting at the age of about two. But you'll notice that saying thanks doesn't always come easily. Very rarely does a kid remember to say it—it usually follows a prompt by a parent...*Now, what do you say?* And it never gets easier.

Gratitude doesn't come easily or naturally to most of us; rather, it's a skill that needs to be honed and crafted. But when you get it down, it can literally change your life. Countless studies have demonstrated that expressing gratitude can vastly increase our physical and emotional well-being.

Gratitude can also have enormous implications for your relationship and your ability to find love if you aren't currently in a relationship. When both partners see the good in one another and feel appreciative, the relationship is filled with love, connection, and harmony. When one or both partners focus on what the other isn't doing and take each other for granted, the relationship is filled with resentment, frustration, and bitterness.

A good relationship starts with you. When you bring positivity and happiness into the relationship, your partner will rise up to match it, and then your relationship will flourish.

If you want your life and your relationship to improve, you can't blame circumstances or your partner. Instead, you need to take responsibility and make internal changes that lead to external ones. And the most important lesson is that of giving thanks.

Why Is It So Hard To Appreciate?

Life can tear a lot of us down. As the years go by, bitter experiences pile up and our hearts become shrouded with hurt and pain. The more jaded we become, the harder it is to see beyond the darkness and feel thankful for anything. A lot of us turn ourselves into victims in the story of our own lives, and we feel justified in doing this: we blame our parents, our upbringing, the boy who broke our heart, the bad economy. I'm not saying none of it is valid, but when you dwell on all the bad hands you've been dealt, you fuel the fire of anger and resentment, and this only makes for an even more miserable experience.

When it comes to relationships, expressing gratitude can be even more challenging because the stakes are so much higher. Romantic relationships can cause many emotions to rise to the surface. Some are good and exhilarating, and some are bad and rooted in pain from the past. All of us look at life through a lens that is colored by our own experiences and we form certain expectations as a result. When you measure a guy against this code of expected behavior, he will always fall short and you will always feel disappointed. The reason he'll fall short is because no one can get it right every single time. He isn't a mind reader, and he has been shaped by a whole different set of experiences.

When you think a guy should do something and if he doesn't it means he doesn't care, then you ignore all the things he is doing to show he cares. You get all riled up because of a few things that you (or rather, your unconscious mind) think a man should do when he loves a woman. You feel hurt and unloved and might start blaming him for "making" you feel a certain way. When you're in this headspace, you will not be able to appreciate anything he does and will silently resent him for not doing more. He can text you back promptly every single time and you will still get upset the one time he takes a little longer to get back to you.

When You Appreciate A Man...

Everyone likes appreciation; we all want to be seen and acknowledged for what we do. But appreciation hits different notes for men and women. Typically, women want to feel adored and cherished above anything else in order to feel happy in a relationship. Men need to feel appreciated and acknowledged. If a man doesn't feel that, he will either leave the relationship or stay in it and feel miserable.

When a man feels like a woman appreciates him, he will go above and beyond to make her happy. It's not just about appreciating what he does, it's about appreciating *who he is*. What a man wants more than anything is a woman who is happy with him. That's really it. And a woman who expresses gratitude and is happy with who he is and what he does is the woman he wants to commit himself to.

The more gratitude you feel for him, the more connected he will feel to you and the more he will come to appreciate you. I'm not saying you're never allowed to be disappointed or upset with him, but there is a difference between disapproving of an action and disapproving of a person. You can express your discontent in a loving way that still conveys an appreciation for his character, as opposed to conveying it in a punishing and blaming way that makes him feel bad or guilty. For example, "I know you didn't mean it, I know you were only trying to be helpful, but sometimes I just need you to hear me out and give me a hug when I'm venting about something upsetting that happened."

The fact is, he really isn't *trying* to hurt you, but sometimes things he does will make you upset. And sometimes things you do will make him upset. When addressing a problem, it's best to keep in mind that neither person is intentionally trying to upset the other.

If you want more love from your man, you need to make him feel loved. The way to do this is to show genuine appreciation for the things he does. Look at the intention, not the action. He's not going to get it right every single time—that just isn't possible. But the majority of the time, his intentions are good. He set out to make you happy, and that deserves to be appreciated. You don't need to give him anything in return; just you being happy with who he is and what he does is all he needs from you.

Here are some examples of emotional hot phrases for a man (obviously they will vary depending on the man):

> I really admire how dedicated you are to your job and appreciate how hard you work.

> You are so committed to causes that are meaningful to you, and it's really admirable.

> I love that you can walk into a room and be best friends with total strangers, it's such a unique gift.

> I appreciate how hard you try to make me happy. I know I don't always show it, but I notice it and it means so much to me.

> Thank you for being so helpful around the house, you really go above and beyond and I don't know what I would do without you.

And if you get stuck...this one is always a winner:

> I admire the man that you are.

How To Train Yourself To Be More Grateful

Now that we've covered why it's important to be grateful, let's talk about tangible ways to do it.

I think the most powerful way to retrain your mind to be more grateful is to keep a gratitude journal. A teacher of mine gave me this suggestion many years ago, and I thought it was the most ridiculous thing I'd ever heard. I considered myself a very grateful person and did not see how it would benefit me at all. But I gave it a try nevertheless, and wow...it was not as easy as I expected. My teacher told me to write down three things I was grateful for every day. Easy enough. The catch was that they always had to be different, as in no reruns.

As the days passed and the exercise got a little more difficult, I noticed myself changing. I started to live every day actively looking for things to be grateful for. Usually this was because I wanted to come up with three things and just be done with it, like getting in an early morning workout. I thought it would only continue to get harder, but a funny thing happened after a few weeks—it actually got easier. And soon, I was finding way more than just three new things to be grateful for each day. I kept going with this for months and can affirm that it is absolutely life-changing. I felt so calm and so at ease and just happier all around.

If you're having trouble in your relationship, I highly suggest you think of two or three things every day that you love and appreciate about your partner. You don't even need to tell him you're doing it or what the things are. Just think about it every day and write it down. And like I did in my exercise, think of new things every day. It can be things he did for you or things about him. Focus on everything he does right, and see how it impacts your relationship. (Mark my word, you'll start seeing major changes within about a week or two.)

Even if you aren't having major issues in your relationship, anytime your partner does something that annoys or frustrates you, just think about a few reasons why you care about him and why you're grateful to have him in your life.

I just want to add that this does not apply to relationships where there is physical or emotional abuse. I'm talking about healthy, functioning relationships that just get rocky from time to time, as most relationships do.

If you're single, think about what you love about your life right now. Think about what you appreciate and the good things that happen throughout the day. I think writing it out is best because it makes it more real, but if that feels like too much of a commitment then just spend time every day reflecting on it.

Practicing gratitude on a daily basis can literally rewire you. It can transform the way you think, which will change the way you feel and the vibe you transmit. People can naturally pick up on the vibes someone is sending out. When you feel bitter or angry or jaded on the inside, it will come across on the outside no matter how you try to hide it. There is no faking being in a good place. You have to work on it, and if you do, suddenly everything will change and you'll notice enormous improvements in all areas of your life.

Remember this: The real way to a man's heart is to appreciate him and empower him. The easiest way to do this is to train yourself to see the good, both in him and in your life in general.

CHAPTER 9

What Pushes Men Away

"Freedom is not the absence of commitments, but the ability to choose—and commit myself to—what is best for me."
—*Paulo Coelho*

Almost every woman has experienced the panic and uncertainty that occur when her man starts pulling away or withdrawing. Maybe it happens out of the blue or maybe something sparks it, but either way it's a miserable feeling, one that leaves you feeling powerless and painfully insecure.

It can happen in the early stages of dating, in an established relationship, or even in a marriage. Suddenly, your sweet, attentive man is a shadow that you can't quite grasp. You try to reach him, but it doesn't work. *Is it something you did? Does he not care about you anymore? Is he losing interest? What is going on?!*

In this section, we are going to look deeper into why men withdraw, pull away, and lose interest and what you can do about it.

Man-Repelling Behaviors

Before we talk about why guys pull away or withdraw, let's talk about some common behaviors that push men away (most of these are people-repellers in general). The one thing I've noticed over the years as a relationship writer is that most women have no idea how they come across to men. They may do things in an attempt to win affection and be completely baffled when their efforts produce the opposite result.

My main source of information for the articles I write is men themselves. Over the years, I've noticed a few recurring themes when it comes to things women do that completely turn guys off.

Here are the top 10 ways to repel a guy:

1. You Brag

Confidence is a major turn-on. Arrogance is not. People are inherently repelled by braggers. I'm sure your efforts are coming from a desire to impress him, but too much showing off will actually repel him. Also, asserting your all-mightiness will make him feel like you're the type of person who will always need to get her way and will never admit to being wrong, and no guy wants to deal with that. Men like their lives easy, comfortable, and drama-free.

2. You're Negative

Having a negative outlook isn't just a man-repeller, it's a people-repeller. We all have our own crap to deal with on a daily basis, and the last thing anyone needs is to get weighed down by someone else's issues and negativity.

3. You Don't "Get" Him

Most men just want to be seen and appreciated. When a man feels this from a woman, he'll want to be around her more. Conversely, when he senses she needs him, or is just trying to get something out of him in order to fulfill her own desire, he will instinctively pull away.

4. You're Critical Or Put Him Down

No one likes to be criticized, but men are particularly sensitive in this area; the male ego is not something to be messed with. A man's greatest need is to feel significant and to feel like a winner in the world. If you make him feel like a loser, he won't want to be anywhere near you.

5. You Fixate On Labels Or A Relationship Status

Men like to be in the moment and they don't want to feel like they're in a relationship pressure cooker where they have to meet deadlines and hit certain marks at the right time or the girl will get upset. Your focus should be on connecting with the other person and determining if this relationship is the right fit, not on getting the title for the sake of having it.

6. You're Manipulative

A guy can sense when he's being manipulated and he'll resent it. Don't do things to intentionally provoke him and get a certain reaction or response from him, this is just immature. Healthy relationships are built on open, honest communication.

7. You're Unhappy

The sexiest woman to a guy is a happy woman. If you hate your life, your friends, yourself, he'll be repelled. Guys like to keep their lives easy and drama-free.

8. You're Unpleasant To Be Around

If a guy feels like hanging out with you is something he's going to have to "deal with" as opposed to something he enjoys, he won't want to do it anymore. A lot of women make the mistake of turning their relationship into a dumping ground where they can unload all their issues. While it's fine to vent to your guy on occasion, if you're constantly going to him to complain about everything in your life then being with you will become a burden.

9. You're Cruel Or Mean To Others

In movies, girls like Regina George are capable of snagging the hottest guy around. In real life, there is nothing sexy about a mean girl; in fact, it's incredibly off-putting. Mean people are generally unhappy people (as they say: hurt people, hurt people). Being mean also reeks of insecurity and emotional issues, two things that no man wants to deal with.

10. You're Combative

It's fine to have opinions and assert yourself as long as you can also see things from the other person's perspective and don't need to be right just for the sake of being right. A lot of women go into relationships seeing their guy as an adversary instead of a partner. The need to fight with him can have a variety of root causes, and your best bet is to identify it and find out what you're really fighting about.

When A Man Needs Space

Few things send a woman spiraling like when a man backs off and takes space. Maybe he comes right out and tells you he needs some space, or maybe you notice he's backing away. You haven't seen him in a while, his texts or calls are shorter and less frequent, and you just feel in your gut that something is amiss.

If you ask him what's going on and why he's being this way, he might come right out and say he needs some space (which does nothing to assuage your mounting anxiety), or he might say something to indicate it in an indirect way, like he needs to focus on work right now, or he's really stressed, or he thinks you should be spending some time focusing on yourself. Even worse, he may pretend like everything is totally normal, making you feel crazy, even though you know you're not crazy and something is just not right here!

A man might ask for space in the beginning of a relationship, or when things are more serious, or even after you're married. No matter what, it's a horrible feeling and you can't stop your mind from spinning and fearing the worst. You try to figure out what you could have done wrong, and you strategize about ways to make things better and get the relationship back on track. This usually doesn't work; if anything it makes the situation even worse.

Here's the thing that's important to realize: men are not women. The way they process and experience things is different. Taking space is a natural coping mechanism for most men, just as seeking out support from friends and loved ones is a natural coping mechanism for most women. Again, we're speaking in generalities.

When a man needs space, it often has little, if anything, to do with you.

But let's get into it a little deeper and look at common reasons and scenarios where men need space, and what you can do about it.

He's Stressed

The number-one reason a man pulls away is because he is stressed. The source of his stress could be the result of some issue in the relationship, but it might not have anything to do with you at all.

Men don't typically like to talk about their problems—they see it as a sign of weakness. A man prides himself on being able to solve issues and can feel extremely unsettled and off balance when problems emerge in his own life that he's not able to resolve. Men will typically view themselves as weak and incapable if they voice their feelings or lean on other people for help or support. A guy might do it, but he'll typically feel like a loser or weakling for asking for support or even talking about his feelings. It's not exactly psychologically healthy, but it is what it is.

To cope with whatever stress he is facing, a man will typically withdraw and go deep into what has become known as a metaphorical "man cave." He will want to hide himself away until he has reached a solution. This doesn't necessarily mean he's sitting down and strategizing about ways to solve the problem. Sometimes he'll just immerse himself completely in something else, like playing video games for hours on end, working, or watching sports.

Men have a much harder time processing and handling emotions than women do. They don't have the same kinds of support systems, and sharing their innermost thoughts and feelings just doesn't come naturally to them. For him, escaping from his feelings temporarily is sometimes more beneficial than trying to sort through them.

What to do: One of the biggest mistakes a woman can make when he's in this mode is to force him to talk about it. Even worse is when she tries to solve the problem for him.

Even though your intentions are pure, when you offer up solutions he feels emasculated. Men need to feel like they are in charge of their lives, like they are capable of solving whatever comes up. He prides himself on being able to solve things, and when you try to do it for him he gets the message that you don't trust that he'll be able to figure it out on his own, and it makes him feel even worse.

When he's under stress, just give him space and try not to take it personally. If you get angry or frustrated with him, he'll just see you as another source of stress in his life, and it will put more strain on the relationship.

Why is this so hard? Even though most women know about the "man cave," they still have a hard time accepting it because women cope with stress very differently. When a woman is upset, she will typically want to talk about it with those she feels closest to. Talking about it is therapeutic, and a solution isn't necessary.

Because of this, if a man doesn't want to talk about his problems, the woman can take it to mean that he doesn't feel close to her, or doesn't fully trust her or care about her. She feels shut out and rejected and may come to resent him for it, thus exacerbating any problems that already exist. It's important to realize that when a man pulls back because he's stressed, he isn't shutting you out. It's just his process, and he will be back and better than ever once he has a handle on whatever is going on.

If he does come to you, don't try to solve the problem for him. Just listen. You can offer advice if he asks, but *only* if he asks.

Space In A Committed Relationship

Another main reason a guy can need to take space in a relationship is if his needs aren't being met or he feels unappreciated. Guys aren't always able to articulate their emotional needs. It could be because they've been conditioned by society not to talk about such things or because they don't have the language to express what they want and need. Some men don't even realize their own emotional deficits, and that is an area where you can be a huge help to him!

A man won't always come right out and tell you what he needs from you, but he will know it when he gets it. So he might not tell you that he really needs your approval and appreciation. Maybe you do show him appreciation, but he needs more and he doesn't know how to tell you that. Instead, he backs away. He isn't as present or engaged, and you feel a palpable space forming and don't know how to break through.

What to do: Try to pay attention to what lights him up and what shuts him down. If he is already deep in the cave, engage in an open, empathetic dialogue and ask him what you could do more of to make him feel good. You might be surprised by what he tells you. And no matter what it is, try not to get defensive. Your instinctive response might be, "I do that all the time!" but try to restrain yourself and hear him out.

You can also voice what you need from him. In any relationship it's important to check in with your partner to make sure both people are happy and getting what they need to feel loved. When you approach him from a place of genuinely wanting to make the relationship better and wanting to make him feel loved, he will be receptive to you.

Space In The Beginning Of A Relationship

Many women have been in situations where they're dating a guy, things are going great, they're spending more and more time together, getting closer and closer...and then he starts pulling away. He might say he needs space, or he might just start taking it without warning. And the woman is baffled. What went wrong? She thought everything was going so well!

These situations usually happen for one of two reasons. The first is a very subtle, sneaky one. It comes from a mindset shift that happens within you. When a relationship starts to get a lot more serious, a lot of women reflexively freak out and become consumed with the fear that things won't work out. This fear causes them to cling tighter to the relationship and to associate their self-worth with how the guy feels. They think about the relationship constantly, obsess over what things mean, and analyze the "signs" looking for bad omens.

The guy can pick up on this energy. Maybe you're being subtle, but he'll feel it on a visceral level. All of a sudden he doesn't feel as relaxed around you, and the vibe is no longer fun and carefree. Instead he feels like he's being analyzed, like something is expected of him, like you don't fully trust him...and it's a bad feeling. He might not be able to pinpoint it, but suddenly he doesn't feel as strong of a pull to be around you.

What to do: Don't stress, everything is fine! Your fears are real; I'm not taking away from that. It could be because you've dated guys in the past who ended it out of the blue, and you're afraid of being in the same situation again. You might not have a solid sense of self-esteem and so you look to men to fill up your self-worth tank. Try to get to the root of this underlying fear so you can internalize that you are lovable and you do deserve lasting love with a great man. (And reread the section on how to stop stressing over your relationship from Chapter 7!)

When It Gets Too Intense, He Will Pull Back

Another likely reason is that he's just freaking out a little bit because things are getting more serious. Many guys worry that a girl will become the gatekeeper of their social calendar as soon as a commitment is made, and they will have to say goodbye to watching football with the guys on Sunday, playing sports, and engaging in every other activity they enjoy. Maybe it sounds stupid and irrational, but it's a real fear for most guys.

A lot of guys have that one friend with a possessive, needy girlfriend he has to check in with every five minutes, and he can't do anything fun. Just that could be enough to scare your guy away, at least for a little bit.

When you give him the space and opportunity to maintain his own life and do what he likes to do, this fear dissipates. Don't stand in the way or make him feel guilty or tell him what he should be doing. Encourage him to be who he wants to be and do what he wants to do, and make sure you do the same. A guy may not always ask for space, but he will be grateful anytime it's granted to him. Giving space isn't an issue if your focus is on making your life an amazing place without needing him to make it that way for you.

And this has benefits for you too. It's also important for you to do your own thing, to spend time on your own or with your friends. When you each have the space to recharge your batteries and re-connect with yourselves and other aspects of your life outside of the relationship, it makes everything better *within* the relationship.

No matter what his reasons for needing space, try not to take it personally and don't harbor resentment towards him over it. Yes, I know you would prefer he talk to you about whatever is going on, but the fact that he doesn't want to is just a sign of how much he cares about you...he cares what you think so much that he doesn't want to come across as weak in your eyes. Try to maintain warm, positive feelings towards him and use the time to focus on yourself and do things that make you feel good.

If you feel really hurt by him taking space, and it's eating away at you, bring it up to him. Just be sure to do it in a loving way, not in an accusatory or attacking way, because that will just make things worse. In the end, remember that when a man needs space, it may have little, if anything, to do with you: He may be stressed out, he may have emotional needs that aren't being met, he may be reacting to clinginess on your part, or he may be worried about losing his freedom. In any of these cases, there are things you can do to reassure him. Focus on those things, and his need for space will no longer be frightening or nerve-wracking. Instead it will be an opportunity to give him something he needs to be his best self.

When He Indirectly Tells You He Needs Space

After about a month of dating, Kara and Mark started spending *all* their time together. They had sleepovers six nights a week and spent every single weekend together. Kara was flattered by the fact that Mark wanted to spend so much time with her and didn't see it as an issue. After a few months of this routine, something funny started to happen. Every few days Mark would say something like, "You know, it isn't good that we spend so much time together, we really should only do sleepovers 3-4 nights a week," Kara usually wouldn't know how to react to this, but it made her feel hurt and rejected.

She was also confused. Mark was the one who initiated all the sleepovers. He was the one always begging to see her. She didn't understand what she could possibly be doing wrong—she was just doing what he wanted. Sometimes when this happened, it would result in a fight, other times just passive-aggressive pouting on her part, but she would always agree and say yes, they did spend too much time together, and a few nights apart would be nice. Then there would be a week of less time spent together, but the following week they were back to spending every night together. He always initiated and she accepted, and like clockwork every few weeks he would express his concern and doubts.

Their relationship became fraught with problems and soon they were always fighting. The only times things were good were when she was able to maintain firm boundaries and take a few nights off. She even did her own thing over an entire weekend and went away with friends, something that had never happened in the eight months they'd been together. But sadly, she would always fall back into the same routine, and it was almost like Mark resented her for being so available...even though *he* was the one initiating.

So what was the problem? Even though men need space and freedom, they don't always know how to go about getting it. When you develop a pattern in the relationship of spending so much time together very early on, a man may also feel that this is what is expected of him, and he's afraid that scaling back will cause problems. Also, Mark did want to spend time with Kara, he loved going to sleep with her and waking up with her in the morning.

But deep down he was also feeling a need for space and freedom. Another issue he had was the fact that they weren't even engaged, yet they were acting like a married couple. This is something else he would bring up to her that she just didn't know how to handle. Essentially, he felt like they were moving too fast, but he didn't know how to find the brakes so he was dragging her along for the ride.

When the terms of a relationship get confusing, a man will oftentimes not know how to respond. This is where *you* need to take the controls and hit the reset button. Mark was clearly (okay, maybe not clearly, but the message was coming across loud and clear in the subtext) telling Kara that he wanted her to do her own thing, but she didn't have the strength to do it.

Why Men Lose Interest

Here is a situation many girls have experienced. You meet a guy and feel the proverbial spark. Numbers are exchanged, flirty texting ensues, and eventually you go on a date...and it's amazing!

The chemistry is strong, you connect, you have fun. You go out again and it's another ace in the hole. Now you start to get really excited...could this be it? Maybe you hang out a few more times and it goes well, but then something changes. Either you notice that he starts to pull away and seems less engaged (commonly known as "the fade-away"), or he just vanishes (a phenomenon known as "ghosting"). You feel completely blindsided and shell-shocked.

What went wrong?

Here is why this situation is so confusing. When a woman loses interest in a guy after a few dates, she can usually pinpoint the reason. Maybe he was too desperate, not intellectually stimulating, too quiet, too loud, too boring, too boisterous—she usually knows exactly what it is that turned her off and can give a reason if asked as to why she doesn't want to continue dating him.

It's not always like this for guys. A guy can go on a few amazing dates with a girl and find himself suddenly and inexplicably put off by her. Whereas he was previously texting her throughout the day and feeling a strong desire to see her...he now has no desire to contact her whatsoever. This can be as baffling for guys as it is for girls. When asked, many guys will say they don't know why they were suddenly turned off; they just were.

So why does this happen? Is it really out of the blue without cause or provocation? No, there is a reason. The reason it's so hard to pinpoint and articulate is because it's extremely subtle.

During the first few dates with a new guy, your vibe is typically pretty laid-back and easygoing. You want to explore the possibilities with him and see what he's all about. It starts out light and fun, and it's about connecting and enjoying each other's company. After a few great dates with a seemingly great guy, most women can't help but get excited about the possibilities. They think of where the relationship might go and they start to invest in a potential future.

When this happens, you are no longer in the here and now, seeing the situation for what it is. Instead, your mind is focusing on what it *could* be and that's when the problem starts. You become attached to this vision and you can't help but stress over it and worry about losing it (even though it's not something you ever really had!) Then your fears and insecurities rise to the surface and seep into your interactions with him.

You begin interacting with the thoughts in your head rather than with the person in front of you. Rather than trying to learn who he is and what he's about, you look at his behavior and the things he says as a means to measure how he feels about you...and whether you're getting closer or further away from your goal of having a relationship with him.

Most guys can intuitively sense when a woman is reacting to them as an object rather than a person, when she is using him as a means to fill a void within herself.

Guys typically don't operate this way in relationships and he can't fully understand what happened to turn this seemingly happy, cool girl into an unpleasant, emotionally-reactive, reassurance-seeking mess.

Why Do We Do This?

All anyone really wants is to feel OK, and most of us don't. When a woman worries and needs constant reassurance, it comes from feeling "I am not OK" and the feeling beneath that is fear. What makes it so destructive is that it's not an overwhelming, gripping fear; it's a vague feeling of unease. It's so quiet and subtle you may not even realize it's there.

It's tough for people to nail down the source of feeling not OK, but they unconsciously latch onto things that will eliminate this feeling, usually through reassurance or trying to make situations come about that they feel will make them happy and finally grant them relief. This inevitably impacts your vibe, you become a parasite of sorts, and everyone you come into contact with is simply a means to an end.

When you meet a guy who makes you feel OK, your need for that feeling becomes overwhelming and you latch on forcefully. You may not even realize you're doing it; it's not something you express outright. But it's there and it comes across, even in the slightest ways. It changes your vibe and your energy, and guys feel this.

At this point, instead of him feeling like he's connecting with you, he feels like you're trying to get something out of him. Maybe it's reassurance or validation, or maybe just more of the feeling of being OK.

Guys don't know exactly what it is, but suddenly their instincts are telling them to get away. This usually occurs at the point where the woman could no longer keep the act up. Maybe she's trying to appear cool and go-with-the-flow, but in her mind she's already thinking of ways to turn a relationship that's really nothing at this point into something. From that point forward, it's not easygoing and natural, it's her measuring if she is getting closer or further from her goal.

Everyone recognizes when someone has an agenda. It's just something our intuition picks up on, and it immediately puts us off.

That's the switch guys feel. It's the shift from things being easy and fun to agenda-driven. When the woman feels like she's getting closer to her goal, she's happy and elated. When something happens that makes her feel like she is moving further away, she is gripped by that, "My world is falling apart" feeling and may try to seek reassurance from the guy, either outright or subtly.

You Can't Force Love

When you take a relationship that is brand new and start thinking that it's something, or try forcing it to be more than it is, it's game over. Your vibe will become man-repelling and before long, he'll be gone and you will be left baffled, analyzing what exactly you did to drive him away. But you won't ever find the answer, because it isn't concrete and measurable.

This is one of the main differences between men and women when it comes to relationships. Men are more in the moment and are able to comfortably enjoy a situation for what it is as it is. Women are always looking for ways to improve the relationship and push it forward. It's not that one gender has it right and the other has it wrong. There needs to be a balance between enjoying the present and comfortably laying the foundation for a future. It just can't be done forcefully.

The best relationships are the ones that unfold organically with two people bringing their best selves to the table and discovering who the other person is and developing an appreciation for that person. It's not about using the other person to gain status or self-esteem or security. A relationship can give you these things, but that's a by-product, not the goal.

This is essentially the difference between a healthy relationship and a toxic relationship. A healthy relationship is one where two people feel fulfilled by their individual lives and let that joy and sense of fullness spill into their relationship. They each bring something to the table and can comfortably give and receive. A dysfunctional relationship is when one or both people believe the other person can "give them" something or that there's something to "get" from the other person.

So what's the solution? If you just enjoy life and engaging with him and make nothing of it, your vibe will still be enjoyable to be around and he will continue hanging out with you. When he feels good around you, he'll want to be around you. When he feels like you're trying to get something out of him, it will push him away.

It's also crucial to get the fear under control. His level of interest is not a life or death scenario, even though it can sometimes feel like your world will actually implode if he leaves you.

A good way to get this under control is to play therapist on yourself. Ask yourself:

> *What am I really afraid of?* I'm afraid he'll lose interest and leave me.
>
> *And then what will happen?* I'll be really sad and depressed.
>
> *And then what will happen?* I'll miss him terribly, it will be awful.
>
> *And then what will happen?* Well I guess eventually I'll pick myself up and move on!

I also want to add that this isn't the *only* reason a man will lose interest; it's just the most common and most misunderstood one. The problem is that most people don't accurately define what the problem is. It gets written off as the woman being too available and not making the guy chase her. That's not really what's at play here. Being available isn't the issue, the issue is really not being present. It's an issue that comes from seeking validation through a relationship rather than in your life.

It is also worth noting that sometimes two people can be happy and satisfied in their lives and just not be a match. Compatibility can't be forced or created, and a lack of it can't be ignored. If you and he are incompatible, it will come to the surface eventually, and a relationship can't last without a foundation of fundamental compatibility.

The winning strategy when it comes to love is to bring your best self to the table and not to stress over your relationship. Instead, trust that if it's right it will work out, and if it's not right you'll be free to move towards something that is the right match for you.

How To Recover From Being "Ghosted" With Your Self-Esteem Intact

Now let's talk about the most painful version of a man disappearing...when he ghosts you. I remember once upon a time it was considered cruel to break up with someone over text but now that's almost the gentlemanly thing to do!

Ghosting is pervasive. I'm sure it's happened to you and if it hasn't and you're still single and dating, then it probably will eventually. It just comes with the territory, unfortunately. Instead of being mad about it, we need to just accept what is and make sure this behavior doesn't put a dent in your self-esteem and leave you bitter and jaded.

Whenever I discuss this topic, I get a strong emotional reaction from my readers. And I fully understand it. It seems immature, it seems childish, and it's just so disrespectful. And how can you not take it personally? He didn't even care about you enough to tell you he no longer wants to see you? So was the whole relationship just a lie, did he never care to begin with?

You feel like a fool; you feel hurt, you feel embarrassed, you feel angry, you have all the bad kinds of feelings, and it's awful.

So let's talk about how to make the experience slightly less awful. I'll try to give you some perspective on why guys "ghost" and how you can move on without feeling bitter and jaded.

I'm going to share the real reasons guys ghost, not the reasons you've convinced yourself of that usually put the blame on you, or on the fact that all men are evil scumbags.

I want to preface this by saying I'm not justifying or excusing the behavior. I'm not saying it's the right thing to do or a nice thing to do. I'm just telling you the plain facts.

1. He Doesn't Want To Have The Uncomfortable Breakup Conversation

Does anyone ever really want to have this conversation? It's the worst. Let's flip things for a minute and see it from a guy's side through a woman's eyes if that makes sense.

So I went on a few dates with a guy we'll call Dan, and I just wasn't feeling it *at all*. And of course, whenever that happens, it means the guy is *totally* feeling it. I knew he would call or text at any moment to ask me out again and my stomach was in knots. I was desperately hoping he would ghost on me so that I wouldn't have to have this conversation.

I didn't want to hurt him. I knew he'd been hurt badly in the past and now I would just be another reason for him to not trust women and to keep himself guarded. I actually got excited when a day went by without me hearing from him. *Maybe he lost interest!! Yes!!!* But I wasn't off the hook, and of course, he called instead to texting to ask me out again so now I'd have to hear his pain on the other end, ugh!

He excitedly asked if I wanted to go apple picking that weekend and I think the last thing in the world he expected was for me to end things. So I told him I just didn't think this was going to work out and he sounded absolutely crushed, and I felt awful.

The reason I'm sharing this is *no one* wants to have this conversation, not guys and not girls. And girls kind of don't have a choice because guys are usually the ones to initiate dates, so we can't just disappear. Some girls do their own version of ghosting by just never replying to a guy when he reaches out again and believe me when I say guys get hurt by this in the same way we get hurt by their disappearances. And in all honesty, I've been that shady girl many a time!

The point is, he just doesn't want to hurt you. He doesn't want to hurt you because he cares about you. Now you might want to counter with: "But that's so immature! He needs to man up!"

So here's the thing, most guys don't decide to ghost. It just kind of happens. He thinks to himself, "Well I don't want to do it today because she has that big project at work, maybe tomorrow." And then tomorrow comes and he has another excuse. Then he thinks it's best to just wait until next week when your emotions have simmered a little bit and you'll maybe be less likely to have a strong emotional reaction.

Then next week comes around and he thinks, "Well it's been so long already, she probably moved on and forgot all about me. It would just be rude of me to call now, she'll probably think I'm a weirdo. I'll just leave this alone..." And so he does.

2. He Thinks You're On The Same Page

The next main reason a guy will ghost is he just assumes you're on the same page as him. He assumes, or maybe he convinces himself, that you know the relationship isn't working. That you also feel the strain or tension. That you also realize that your values are different or that your personalities are totally different or that you two are fundamentally incompatible or whatever the case may be.

He thinks that you probably already know it's not working out, so why does he really need to call and tell you? That will just be weird and awkward, so best to just leave it alone.

That's how I felt with Dan. I was almost shocked that he seemed so blindsided because didn't he realize how incompatible we were?

Usually only one person gets the clarity. Sometimes you see that it's not a match, sometimes he sees it. And sometimes you get lucky and you both see it and can part amicably.

3. The Relationship Wasn't What You Thought

Sometimes, we end up in one sided relationships. Sometimes we care significantly more than the other person does and we blind ourselves from the reality of the situation because we want him to like us back so badly.

In your mind there is a lot of potential here, in your mind this could really be something special. But in his mind, you're a girl he was somewhat interested in, you had a very casual relationship and it wasn't really going anywhere and he didn't think it warranted an official "breakup conversation."

He may have liked you, but he didn't like you enough to want a relationship with you. Even if he did come right out and say it to your face, would that really have hurt any less?

Sometimes it just isn't a match. That's just the reality of dating and compatibility.

This is usually the case for very short-lived relationships, like a few dates max, where he didn't have the time to really develop strong feelings.

4. He Has An Avoidant Attachment Style

If things were going amazingly well and then all of a sudden there was a dramatic shift, it's possible he has an avoidant attachment style and a core wound around affection and intimacy that got activated and scared him off.

I know it's incredibly frustrating when this happens because you saw so much potential, but his wounds are his problems to deal with. It is possible to have a relationship with an avoidant person, but they need to manage their emotional damage and heal on their own, otherwise the relationship will always be on shaky, unstable ground and that's just not fair to you.

Now Let's Talk About How To Recover With Your Self-Esteem Intact

1. Realize It's Not Because You Were Insignificant

The biggest mistake women make is assuming a guy ghosted because she meant nothing to him, because he never really cared about her, or because she wasn't even worth a breakup text.

This isn't reality, these are your deepest fears talking. See most of us have deeply rooted fears of being unlovable or unworthy. It's sad and unfortunate and way too common. The unconscious mind is always looking for ways to prove itself right so when something like this happens, it shouts: "See? I told you that you were unworthy!" But there is no relief that comes from this confirmation.

Feelings aren't facts. Just because you feel like this has to be the case doesn't mean it is. If you adopt the idea that he ghosted because you were meaningless and easily forgettable, you're only dooming yourself and blocking yourself from getting the love you want. And remember: *two things can be true at the same time.* It can be true that he did really like you, he just didn't think it would work out.

Most men are good at compartmentalizing. They can just put their feelings in a box and shove that box deep into the recesses of their mind. It may seem like they never cared on the outside, but really they did, they just don't dwell on the care. They can reason that it didn't work out, it wasn't going to work out, so what's left to think about?

2. Don't Reach Out To Him

He already left, don't let him take your dignity with him. When these things happen, a woman will often convince herself she needs to reach out because she "needs" closure.

The closure never ever comes from reaching out to him. You know what usually does come? More silence. You send him a well thought out text that you wrote and rewrote a hundred times. You hit all the right notes. You make sure you sound mature, composed, cool, and confident. You explain that you just want an explanation and feel he owes you one after the time you spent together. But he doesn't feel the same it seems...and he ignores you.

Why does he do that? Men have a strong aversion to getting into emotionally heavy conversations. If men had their way the only emotions they would ever experience are calm and contentedness. When a man senses an emotional maelstrom brewing, he won't go anywhere near it. Does that make it right? No, but just look at me as your tour guide through male brain world and not as a lawyer making a case for why this is acceptable behavior.

Sometimes you need to make your own closure. He won't give it to you. Closure means it's closed, it's done. You don't need him to give you that.

And let's say he does reply to your beautifully worded, well thought out text. Do you think he's actually going to tell you the real reason he doesn't want to see you anymore? He won't. He's going to say something else. He's too busy, he's stressed, he's not ready for a relationship right now. He's not going to say the real answer, which is he just doesn't like you enough to put in the effort for a relationship.

On that note...

3. Not Everyone Is A Match And That's Ok

It feels personal but it's not. It doesn't mean you're fundamentally flawed, it just means you're not the right person for him. Maybe you disagree, but it takes two people to be in a relationship, and if one of those people doesn't want it, then you have nothing.

Rather than dwelling on all the things that must be wrong with you to make you such a man-repeller, focus on the fact that he just wasn't the right guy for you because the right guy for you *wants to be with you.*

Guys can lose interest for all sorts of reasons. And if a guy loses interest over something small, he was never really all that interested in the first place. If a guy really likes you, like *really likes you,* it will take a hell of a lot to convince him out of it. He is in it and he's not going anywhere.

4. Stay Busy

As they say, idle hands are the devil's plaything. If you stay home and sulk and feel sorry for yourself you'll allow your mind to steer you to all sorts of dark places and this is highly counterproductive. This will just crush your self-esteem and make you more guarded and jaded which will make it even harder to form a genuine connection when a decent guy comes along.

Try to stay busy and positive. Do things you enjoy that make you feel really good. Surround yourself with people who love you and see the best in you. Make time for your passions and for things that make you feel alive, charged, and revitalized.

Eventually, you will find that right guy and when you do, all of this will make sense, and you'll be tempted to write all the ghosts from your past thank you notes for not wasting anymore of your time than they did!

How To Be Charming & More Likable

Everybody wants to be charming. When you see someone who seems to easily captivate the attention of anyone in a room, it's natural to want to emulate that. While it can seem like something that you either have or you don't (and yes, for some people it does come more naturally) the reality is you can learn how to be more charming and likable.

1. Be Genuinely Interested In Others

Showing off and talking yourself up isn't charming, being genuinely interested in other people is.

It feels good when someone shows an interest in your life. When a person is categorically curious about you, it makes you feel special. You can do this for other people by asking questions about their life—their job, hobbies, and family.

Being charming isn't so much about what you're doing, it's how other people feel around you.

Try to listen more than you speak—don't just wait for your turn to say something.

2. Remember Their Name And Use It Often

Dale Carnegie, author of the massively successful book "How to Win Friends and Influence People," said "Remember that a person's name is to that person the sweetest and most important sound in any language."

Pay attention to anytime someone uses your name often in a conversation, there is something intoxicating about it!

Using someone's name carries a real impact. On a basic level, it lets the other person know that they are significant enough for you to remember and confidently use their name. If they are not fully invested in a conversation with you, using their name will be a tug that brings you into focus.

When you remember someone's name, and use it in conversation, it just makes them feel special. And the most basic principle to be charming is to make people feel good around you.

3. Talk About Yourself Without Talking Yourself Up

Bragging is just gross, same with humble bragging. Being charming isn't about making people feel envious of you—it's making people feel comfortable and happy and even inspired around you.

When you brag, it comes across like you have something to prove and this is always a turn off, whether on a date or a job interview or even just meeting someone new.

While you want to make sure the majority of a conversation is not about you, it's still a good idea to share a few things. If you avoid spilling any personal information, you will come across as cold and overly guarded. The fastest way to make someone else feel comfortable being vulnerable is to open up yourself.

4. Smile

A smile is completely disarming. Smiling immediately puts people at ease and conveys that you have friendly intentions.

However, it needs to be genuine. Everyone knows that smiling is powerful so you can't just plaster on a fake smile. A fake smile stops at the mouth, a real smile extends all the way up to the eyes.

Try to just let go a little bit— find the humor in everything, don't be afraid to smile and laugh freely—this just puts people at ease and they in turn will do the same.

5. Have Open Body Language

Charming people have a way of making you feel like the most important person in the room. They make eye contact, they stand facing you, they are engaged with what you're saying, and give you their undivided attention.

6. Be Playful

Charming people are usually energetic and bubbly; watch an interview with Jennifer Lawrence to see this in action.

They don't try to minimize themselves to be on the same level as someone else. They let their energy and positivity shine and this is infectious and lifts the other person up as well.

7. Make People Feel Good

The reason why charming people are so beloved is they have a way of making others feel really good. But they aren't fake about it, they are able to be real and genuine and this is what really strikes a chord.

This doesn't mean you suck up to them and pour on the compliments, this is just creepy and will make people suspicious of you.

It's about showing genuine interest in the other person—and recognizing their strengths and what you might have to learn from them.

8. Don't Talk Badly About Other People Or Be Negative

This is just the sign of a jealous, unhappy person. There isn't a reason to trash someone else and if you do need to vent, there is always a nicer way to get your feelings out

Negativity is also a trap. For whatever reason, it feels good to lean into that toxic headspace but it's not good for you and it doesn't feel good to be around you when you surrender to those feelings.

Our mood can be contagious. Ever been around someone who was extremely stressed? All of a sudden you become stressed, your breathing pattern may even start to match theirs and now you just want to get away!

9. Be Confident

Charming people are confident. They know they can navigate any situation and don't question or doubt themselves. They also don't play the game of thinking back to everything they said in a conversation and flinching in regret or something dumb they said. Most people do this but here is the thing: people don't remember what you said, they remember how you *made them feel*. So stop replaying every interaction that didn't unfold perfectly!

When you are confident, you are comfortable with who you are which makes you charming and makes people want to be around you.

Remember this: If a guy takes space or ghosts, don't take it personal. It's more about him and his process. The best thing you can do is back off and continue working on your feelings of worth and happiness.

CHAPTER 10

How to Communicate

"*Healthy relationships*...Let's not forget it's you and me vs. the problem...NOT you vs. me." —*Steve Maraboli*

We've talked a lot in this book about how to attract the right relationship...but what happens when you're in it?

Good communication skills are vital to succeed in any area of life, especially relationships. Unfortunately, it's not always the easiest skill to master. In relationships, both romantic and not, it's not so much what you say, it's the *way* you say it that makes all the difference. Saying the right words in the right way can lead to a closer connection and increased happiness for both people. Saying things in the wrong way can cause massive fights and mounting resentments.

Communicating well during a heated argument is an art of its own, but what really makes all the difference is the day-to-day communications. It's about how you express your needs, show your appreciation, and express love to your partner in the way he most feels it. While this chapter focuses on communicating in a romantic relationship, these communication skills can be used in all areas of your life.

Getting A Man To Do Anything For You

Here is a common relationship scenario that any woman who has ever been in a relationship has most likely experienced.

Your guy isn't doing something you want him to do (and know he's capable of doing). You call him out on it and he withdraws, and not only does he not do the thing you asked, he may even do the opposite.

For instance, let's say a guy was a texting machine in the beginning of the relationship, but then as the relationship progressed, the number of daily texts started to drop.

The girl really misses the good old days of constant texts. She knows he's capable of it, she's unhappy that he no longer does it, so in her mind the logical thing to do is say something to him about it.

So she says, "Why don't you text me all the time like you used to?" thinking that she's sending her message loud and clear. And she is, right?

Well, when she says this to a guy, he feels like a failure. He feels like he isn't living up to her expectations and as a result, he feels defeated.

It may not even be conscious on his part. It's a feeling that emerges beneath the surface and manifests as him withdrawing or continuing to do the thing that bothers you.

So what's the solution?

It's pretty simple and if you can master it, you will never again feel frustrated by your man.

The solution is to *empower* him by encouraging the kinds of behaviors on his part that make you happy and make you love and desire him, rather than demanding that he be a certain way and pointing out the ways in which he's failing to make you happy.

If a man feels that his girl respects, appreciates, and can happily receive what he has to give, he will do anything to keep her happy.

So how do you do this? Well this is the tricky part. It isn't about something you should say or do in order to get him to do what you want. That's just manipulative, and if that's the place you're coming from, he'll sense it and it will make things worse.

The kind of woman who gets the unwavering attention and affection so many other women crave from their partners is the one who is in a good place emotionally.

She doesn't demand anything from him and she doesn't need anything from him.

Instead, she sees and appreciates him for who he is, and she is OK if there are times when he doesn't do exactly what she wants. This, in turn, makes him want to go above and beyond for her.

When a woman is unstable, or carrying hurt/pain/insecurities, she will pressure her man to act a certain way in order to feel better about the situation, not because she actually needs him to text five times a day.

If a woman is holding onto these pains and fears, she isn't coming from a place of love, she's coming from a place of needing to control her man and the relationship or her self-esteem will suffer.

Men never ever respond well to demands, and they want to be *wanted*, not *needed.*

The point I'm making (and have been making throughout this book) is that it's vital to work on yourself and get to a strong place internally, a place where you can receive what he has to give, not a place that makes you feel empty and alone when he doesn't do every single thing you want exactly the way you want him to.

Emotional development takes work, so here is a helpful way to know if you're coming from a place of neediness so you can hopefully begin to work on it.

When you feel disappointed/frustrated/angry by something your guy is doing and you try to force him to change, you should ask yourself if you're doing it for him or for you.

For instance, if you want your guy to be more emotionally supportive, ask yourself if you want this because it would be beneficial for him in his life to be more sensitive, or is it because you need it in order to feel more confident in the relationship because you're feeling unstable or insecure and need his reassurance in order not to feel abandoned?

Going back to our previous example, why is it that you want him to text more often?

Is it because you feel that being in constant communication will strengthen the relationship and make it better for both of you, or is it because you're unsure about his feelings and use his texts as a barometer for how he feels?

If you can step back and examine your true motivations for wanting something out of your guy, you will gain important insight into yourself.

You will also create space to see the situation more objectively and will be better able to act without pushing your guy away.

The Magic Formula

When it comes to communicating with men, there is a simple magic formula that is so powerful it can literally transform your entire relationship into one that is happier and more filled with love than you ever imagined.

I was talking to a friend the other day who is having a hard time with her husband. She doesn't feel he is affectionate enough with her and wishes he would give her compliments and words of affirmation more often. She said every time she brings it up, he gets defensive and angry and counters by saying he does do those things for her and he's trying his best, but when she doesn't acknowledge him for it and instead keeps telling him he isn't doing enough, it makes him want to stop trying.

This is a common issue any woman in a relationship is bound to run into. The reason is that we often don't know how to speak in a language that our man will hear and understand. And that's because it's a tough thing to do, especially when we're feeling hurt or upset by his behavior.

The truth is, men are easy creatures. It's very easy to get your guy to treat you the way you want to be treated, you just have to go about it the right way. If you go about it the wrong way, he will become the most stubborn, difficult person you have ever encountered.

And the right way to communicate with a man is as follows:

Whenever you need something from your guy, frame it using this formula:

Praise, Request, Thanks.

Here are some examples:

> "You are such a great guy and I know you wouldn't intentionally hurt me, because you never do things to intentionally hurt me. I really would appreciate it if you could be a little more supportive and encouraging because this is a stressful time for me. Thank you so much for always being there and always trying, I really appreciate it."

> "You are so loving and do so much for me. I really love it when you show me affection and give me compliments. If you could be more affectionate, it would make me feel even more loved by you. I know that being affectionate and complimentary doesn't come naturally to you, so thank you so much for trying and for realizing this is important to me."

> "You are such a go-getter and are so amazing at your job, and the success you have achieved is incredible. I know you're very busy at work, but I would love it if you could try to

> call or text me more often during the workday, because it makes me feel good when I hear from you. I really appreciated it the other day when you took the time to call me even though you had back-to-back meetings. I noticed it, and it made me feel really good that you took time out of your day to check in with me."

You get the gist. It sounds simple on paper, but I know that when you're angry with him, or hurt, it can be really difficult to summon this sort of compassion. Instead, you may subconsciously want to hurt him back and make him feel really bad because he's making you feel bad.

You need to realize that this approach gets you absolutely nowhere. When you frame things like, "Why don't you ever compliment me/appreciate me/support me/call me? I do everything for you and you can't even do the little things I need, and it's not fair!" his defenses will immediately go up, and nothing you say will penetrate. Instead, he'll say that you don't appreciate him, you don't respect him, you're being unreasonable...which will make you even more upset and cause you to lash out even more... which will make him even more defensive and accusatory...and the resentments, hurt, and anger will continue to mount.

In relationships, most women primarily need to feel loved and cared for while most men need to feel appreciated and significant. When you focus on what he's doing wrong and make him the bad guy, he feels like he's failing you, and this will make him less motivated to give you what you want. It's the same as when he isn't doing things that make you feel loved, and then you're less loving towards him, or less inclined to show him appreciation.

Relationships aren't a quid-pro-quo exchange; they're not about keeping score or going tit-for-tat. When you take that approach you will always lose. Maybe you're totally right, maybe he isn't affectionate enough for you, but although proving this with a list of examples may win you the battle, you will lose the war because your relationship will suffer.

Men are highly, *highly* sensitive when it comes to criticism and rejection. He doesn't want to feel like a bad guy who is incapable of making you happy. The one thing he wants more than anything in a relationship is to see you smile. So when you have an issue to bring up with him, it's also important that you don't frame it as him being the problem. For example, saying something like, "You're so insensitive and I can't deal with it!"

Again, making him feel bad about himself won't get you anywhere. It's also not a nice thing to do to someone you love. Instead, you can say, "I'm really stressed right now and that's not your fault; I just don't handle stress very well, and in stressful times I need some extra love and support from you."

That is so much better than saying, "Can't you see how stressed I am? Why can't you just support me instead of being so difficult?!"

Believe me, I know how difficult it can be to do this when you're feeling hurt or overwhelmed or stressed. If you can't summon an ounce of love or compassion in that moment, then don't address the issue until you are able to get out of that emotional whirlpool. This could take ten minutes, a few hours, or a few days. However long it takes, try not to bring up the issue until you are able to do it from a place of equanimity.

Emotions can be contagious. If you come at him from an angry, accusatory place, he will feel defensive and then will also be angry and accusatory, and then nothing will get resolved and no one will be happy.

In a relationship, it's always important to try to see the good. There will always be some bad because no one is perfect, not him and not you. What you choose to focus on is what makes all the difference.

You can choose to dwell on his flaws and all the little ways he isn't making you happy, or choose to see the good, to appreciate him for the things he is doing, which in turn will make him want to do even more. It's like those artsy photographs where there is a beautiful flower in focus and everything else is blurry. In relationships, try to adjust your lens so the flower is in focus and shines brighter than the other stuff.

Remember, all it takes is praise->request->thanks. If you frame what you need in that way, you will notice he becomes a whole new man, and your relationship will become a much happier, more loving place.

Rules To Obey When You Argue

Conflicts are a built-in part of any relationship. No two people, no matter how perfectly matched, will get along in perfect harmony at all times. One of the greatest accomplishments in my relationship with my husband is not that we never argue, but that we argue so well (which actually means that we're good at resolving our conflicts).

This was not the case earlier in our relationship, especially not when we were engaged. Back then if we went two days without a fight it was cause for celebration. We used to fight bad and dirty. Petty disagreements would spiral into all-out war. It wasn't pretty, and there were times I wondered if we were going to make it. Sometimes in the midst of an argument it felt like we were speaking two totally different languages, completely unable to comprehend what the other was trying to say.

One of the most essential skills for a couple to master is learning how to argue well. We both had to do some work to get to a place where we could disagree peacefully, but ever since we got married we hardly ever argue. When we do, we're able to resolve it in record time, and afterwards our relationship is usually even stronger than before. That's the thing about conflict: when handled right, your relationship can strengthen. When done wrong, you each can start holding onto resentment and this can erode any happy, loving feelings within the relationship.

So let's talk about the right way to argue. First, it's important to remember that arguments are a chance to grow, and that you and your partner are fighting for the same cause (to reach a place of love and harmony). He's not your enemy and you're not his, so above all else make sure to enter into the interaction from a place of unity so it's each of you facing a conflict together, not each of you pitted against the other.

1. Respond Instead Of Reacting

Learning the distinction between responding and reacting will help your relationship enormously, and it's also a very valuable life skill. I remind myself to respond instead of react many, many times throughout the day when dealing with my small children!

When you respond, you are in control; you get to weigh your options and determine how you feel and how you would like to handle the situation. You don't blame the other person for "making" you feel a particular way, because you are in the drivers seat.

When you react, they have complete control. You may say things you don't mean, feel things you don't want to feel. You go on instinct and may regret how you reacted. Reacting rarely takes things in a positive direction. Your knee-jerk reaction may be anger and indignation, or you may try to get back at the other person.

Learning to respond instead of react sounds great in theory, but it can be really difficult in practice, especially when things are heated. You are really going to have to gain control of your mind to do this right.

Just remind yourself that you get to choose how to respond to what's happening; you don't need to be controlled by your immediate reactions, which may only be manifestations of anger in the moment, anger that will soon dissipate. When you cave to these fleeting emotions, the conflict will only continue to escalate.

I don't expect you or anyone to stop having negative thoughts. Even after years of practice I can't do that, and there's no sense in beating yourself up over there. What any person *can* do is choose not to *feed into the negativity*. Even if you have a negative thought or negative initial reaction, just accept that it happens and make a solemn decision not to feed into it. When you can do that, then the rest of the good habits will take hold and conflict patterns will dissolve.

2. Take A Step Back

This is part of learning to respond instead of react. If things start to get really heated, tell your partner that now just isn't a good time to talk about whatever the issue is and you'd like to discuss it later. In the meantime, you should take a walk, go to the gym, or just go someplace where you can be by yourself to let things settle down and gain some more clarity and perspective.

In moments of anger we all kind of turn into two-year-olds throwing a tantrum. We can't see beyond our own pain and the anguish of the moment. Toddlers can be perfectly happy one minute, laughing and giggling and everything is great, but then something happens and it's like the whole world is ending. All they can feel is the pain of the moment and a crushing disappointment because the happiness from two minutes before no longer exists.

In a heated exchange, you might totally forget that this person in front of you is someone you love, someone you're sharing a life with, someone you admire. All you see is that he's being stubborn or difficult and making your life hard, and all the good within him disappears. Maybe he is being a huge jerk and maybe he does deserve your wrath, but conversations during moments of anger or extreme emotion rarely go in a positive direction. Instead, things typically escalate and worsen.

Like I said earlier, you're on the same team, and the goal is to get along and reestablish that connection you share. As soon as you step away from a situation, you might see things in a whole new light; something that seemed like the end of the world a few minutes earlier might not be that big of a deal.

3. Get To The Root Of The Problem

The reason a lot of couples get into the cycle of endless arguing is because they don't address the root of the problem. Instead they argue about trivial things instead of the *real* thing.

One big complaint women have is that their guy doesn't help out at all, and they have to do everything. They may have a fight over him not taking out the garbage or leaving dirty dishes in the sink, but they aren't addressing the core issue. Maybe they'll argue that not taking the garbage out will attract bugs and rodents (a valid argument!), but that isn't the point. The point is the woman most likely feels taken for granted and maybe like her man doesn't care for her. That's what's really going on.

Whenever you have recurring arguments, or find yourself going at it over something that seems trivial, try to uncover what you're really upset about.

Also realize that not every problem is meant to be solved. Sometimes you just need to accept certain things as they are, within reason of course.

4. Don't Fight Dirty

In a moment of anger, it's tempting to jab your opponent between the ribs, but it isn't helpful and will only make things worse! Try not to resort to name-calling, labeling, and attacking to get your point across. Also, stay away from over-generalizations. ("You never do anything for me." "You always leave things lying around.) No one ever *always* or *never* does something, and I'm sure anytime someone used an always or a never on you it was infuriating. It's right up there with someone telling you to "calm down."

Name-calling is also problematic. Yes, it may have been in a moment of anger, but once you say it you can't unsay it, and you don't know how it's going to hit your partner and affect him. Instead of "You're such a jerk," you can say, "You were acting like a jerk." Just that small little tweak makes a difference because people always get defensive when they are given a negative label.

Even though your partner might be making you insane, remember that he isn't *all bad*. If he were, you wouldn't be with him (hopefully). He's actually someone you like and love, and we should never intentionally try to hurt the people we care about. That's destructive and can lead to a toxic relationship.

5. Remember That Being Sorry Is Better Than Being Right

Look, I know what it feels like when you are so frustrated with your partner and basically want to wring his neck because you are so right and he is so wrong. How can he possibly not realize how incredibly stupid and wrong he is and how he makes no sense? And you make so much sense it's insane!

All you want is to prove that you're right because...you are right! And maybe you are. But when you get locked in this kind of battle you both lose because you become opponents; you're fighting against each other, and the other person becomes your enemy. And if you're in a fight, then chances are he thinks you're wrong, and chances are, he's probably right. He's probably a little wrong and a little right, just like you're a little wrong and a little right.

What will get you to a place of understanding and resolution is to not try to win and prove who's right, it's to be sorry that your partner was hurt (even if he was wrong). It sucks to be the first to apologize (and if you're always the first to apologize that is a sign that something is amiss in the relationship, and it should definitely be addressed because not being able to take responsibility is a major red flag). You don't want to apologize; you don't think he deserves it, and maybe he doesn't. But no matter what, no matter how justified you are, you can still be sorry that he is hurt, or sorry that you said something you shouldn't have. Because when you love someone, you don't ever want to hurt him or cause him pain.

In a moment of conflict it may not feel that way, but overall, that's where you're coming from (hopefully, anyway). Trying to prove your case won't get you anywhere. Showing empathy and compassion and owning up to whatever your share in the conflict was will usually get the other person to do the same. Yes, I know it's annoying to be the bigger person, but someone has to do it; otherwise you'll be forever locked in a battle of wills, and no relationship can survive in that state.

You can't win every argument, and some conflicts will never be solved. You just need to respect each other and respect your differences.

How To Get More Love From Him

I'm going to share the secret to getting more love from your guy and that is...be lovable!

I know, I know, it sounds pretty revolutionary. But here's the thing, I don't think a lot of us realize the kind of energy we're putting out there and into our relationships.

Relationships have a way of bringing all our unresolved crap to the surface. And sometimes, we may unknowingly use our relationship as a dumping ground for everything that's bothering us. We may also take our frustrations out on our partner (the same way we did with our parents when we were younger) because those feelings need to be unleashed somewhere!

It's far easier to get mad at your guy for not being emotionally supportive about how horrible your boss is than to get into a fight with your boss about how mean she is.

I'm not saying you shouldn't ever vent or share your feelings in your relationship. You can and you should, as long as you don't turn personal problems into relationship problems. You need to have a handle on your own life so you don't let negativity from the outside seep into the relationship. The way to do this, for example, is to vent about what's going on, then lovingly thank your guy for listening and do something sweet for him. This will enhance the amount of love in your relationship whereas yelling at him for not being more sympathetic to your situation will just make things worse.

When you allow negativity to seep into your mind and body, you transmit a highly unattractive vibe. I remember a point during my engagement where I was literally my ugliest internal self. Even though I was planning a wedding to get married to the most amazing man I've ever known, I was spouting negativity end to end. I was stressed and overwhelmed (and the roaches!) and I would complain to anyone who would listen, especially my guy. And I was always mad at him for something. Sometimes it was justified, other times I was just taking things out on him.

One night we decided to go out on a date, something we hadn't done in months! I had decided earlier that day to release all my negativity and just enjoy doing something fun for a change. That decision completely changed everything. My guy even noticed something looked different about me when we met up. We had an incredible night and I felt more love and connection than ever before.

At the end of our date I thanked him for being so loving and he replied "Thank you for being so lovable." I was pretty awestruck. That's all it takes? That's how easy it is? And in that moment, a concept I have written about countless times really got hammered in: all a man really needs in a relationship is for the woman he's with to be thoroughly happy.

You can certainly vent to him when you have a lot going on, but it's important to do it in a way where you don't make him feel like the problem and you let him know how much you appreciate having him there to listen.

Men don't always realize that just hearing a woman out serves a purpose and helps her feel better. For example, when you see him after a hard day don't unleash a litany of complaints on him or an itemized list of all the things that went wrong that day, first tell him how happy you are to see him, how it's been a tough day but being with him makes it better. Let him know his presence is the solution in your life, and then you can share what happened with him.

The takeaway message is this: getting angry at your guy for not being as loving as you want will not fill him with loving feelings towards you. What makes him feel loving is when you are lovable.

And now we're going to come full circle. In order to be lovable you *must* love yourself. There is no other way. And that is at the root of what creates an amazing, happy, loving relationship. That should be your focus more than anything else. That is what makes all the difference. And that is what will change everything and open the door to getting the love you've always wanted.

Remember This: Be on the same team as your man; he is your ally, not your adversary. When you have this mindset you will defeat any conflict rather than allowing the conflict to defeat you.

Final Thoughts

Well, we made it to the end, and I hope you enjoyed the journey! I hope after completing this book you no longer feel the urge to overthink everything in your relationships. I hope you can finally *enjoy* your relationships without *stressing* and second guessing and questioning yourself and worrying. I hope you've gained clarity, both on why men act the way they do as well as why *you* act the way you do in relationships. Maybe you've even discovered some unhealthy patterns and habits and learned the tools to break them.

If you were blocked from receiving love, I hope you were able to release whatever you were holding onto that held you back from being able to love freely and receive love without suspicion. I hope you feel empowered and excited to start a new journey, one where you put your focus on building your self worth, because by now you know how important that is.

It is a lifelong journey and commitment. There is no finish line to cross. Every day you have to make the choice to fill yourself up. You have to choose to be happy, and this choice consists of a bunch of mini-choices we make throughout the day. You have to make the choice every day to believe you are worthy and to treat yourself with love and care. When you do this, everything else will fall into place.

I heard an idea recently from Mel Robbins that had a profound impact on me: happiness comes from making the harder choice. For example—when your alarm sounds in the morning, the easy choice is to hit snooze and just go back to sleep. The harder choice is getting out of bed at the crack of dawn, getting in a workout or a meditation, checking your emails, and getting organized to have a productive day. The second choice is harder, but it will increase your feelings of happiness because you are nourishing yourself and setting yourself up for success.

Happiness isn't just going to happen. It takes effort. But the good news is, the more you make the choice, the more you exert the effort to be happy, the easier and more natural it will become and eventually you will just be an overall happier, more fulfilled person.

I was 23 and single as can be when I started A New Mode. I was essentially clueless. I started writing about my failed relationships because I thought others would relate. I never thought this would turn into a career as a relationship writer and coach but here we are over a decade later.

Now I'm a tad older and married and a much more refined, savvy, self-aware version of my former self. Of course the journey never ends, there's always so much more to learn. Being married and becoming a mother has opened a new door for me in many ways and given me a whole new arsenal of topics to write about.

I hope you feel clear and empowered, and that you get and keep that love you've always wanted by being your true and absolute best self. Stay in touch!

sabrinabendory.com
thoughtcatalog.com/sabrina-bendory
tiktok.com/@sabrinabendory

Lots of love,
Sabrina Alexis Bendory

P.S. You should now be equipped with everything you need to know to find and keep love that lasts. We covered a lot in this book, and I want all the material to really stay with you, to penetrate and make the kind of difference that will allow you to get and keep a happy, loving, mutually fulfilling relationship. So here is a little refresher course before we say goodbye. I've pulled the most important information from each chapter and elaborated on why it's such a life-changer.

If you find yourself struggling with a situation that you don't know how to handle, but don't have time to reread this entire book, use the following cheat sheet to get you quickly back on track!

Cheat Sheet

1. Choose Wisely

I spent far too many years wondering why my relationships always fell apart and I couldn't get anything to last. The answer was so obvious I felt like a fool for failing to see it all along: I was choosing the wrong men. I was choosing the men who wouldn't or couldn't give me what I wanted. When I finally wised up and started dating with more of a purpose, dating with the aim of finding something long lasting instead of dating around just for the sake of dating around, I cultivated a new mantra: I want a partner, not a project.

When it hit me it changed my life. I had spent so many years trying to cure these damage cases who would have been terrible lifelong partners! What a colossal waste of time and energy. I didn't want someone I had to fix. Yeah, the challenge could be invigorating, but life is exhausting enough, why make it even more complicated? You need to date selectively. You need to have a firm sense of what you want and need and don't compromise... no matter how sexy and mysterious he is!

2. Love Is Amazing... But It Isn't A Fantasy

Love won't make all your pain and problems go away. It won't erase the memory of all your old hurts and wounds, it won't give you a healthy sense of self-esteem, and it won't open the gates of everlasting happiness and bliss. Love can enhance your life in many ways (healthy love, that is), but it will never be perfect. There is no such thing as a perfect partner or a perfect relationship.

This one took me a while to fully grasp because like many women, I fell for the popular ideology our culture perpetuates about love. I thought that with the right person, it would all just work out and everything would be amazing. I thought love was enough. But it isn't. It's also about timing (it has to be the right time for both people), fundamental compatibility, similar goals, and emotional maturity. Love can be a beautiful, transformative thing, but not in a vacuum. A lot of other elements need to align, and you need to accept and embrace the fact that it will take a bit of work.

3. Sometimes You're The Problem

Being single for an extended amount of time can be for two reasons: you legitimately haven't met the right guy, or you aren't yet the right girl. I dated my husband in high school and we ran into each other countless times over the span of a decade. Our last chance meeting was two months before we actually started dating again. For whatever reason when he saw me that day in Central Park, he wasn't overcome with a desire to ask me out. Then two months later he was. By our second date he knew I was "the one."

So what changed? Nothing changed about me physically, but I'd spent that entire summer really working on myself. I focused on friends and fun and getting to the root of some of my long-standing issues. I'm not saying this is exactly why he asked me out, but I just don't think it's a coincidence that once I was in this amazing, empowered place, he plopped back into my life (and is now stuck in it for the long haul!) I'm not saying it's your fault, but we could all stand some self-improvement; making some tweaks can help turn us into our best selves, the self that is capable and worthy of attracting the love we've always wanted.

4. Stop Wasting Time!

Oh, what I would do to get back some of the time I've wasted over the years on total losers. If he won't be your boyfriend, if he won't commit, if he treats you badly, if he doesn't appreciate you, if he only appreciates you for sex and can't be bothered when you're fully clothed, forget him. It seems so obvious, yet so many of us fail in this area. Why does it happen?

Essentially, a lot of us are programmed to view ourselves as the problem. We think if only we were better, if we tried harder, if we gave more, then everything would work out. When you make yourself the problem, you can stay stuck in a dead-end relationship for years. Forget the wasted time, think about what that does to your self-esteem. I spent a year obsessing over a guy that I never actually dated! OK, we went on two dates, then he ended it saying he didn't think we were "right for each other," but I couldn't let it go. We would still hang out, still hook up, and each time I would be filled with a renewed sense of hope...until it would all come crashing down and I would once again be left sad and disappointed, wondering what I was doing wrong and why he didn't want to be with me.

But I wasn't the problem, the problem was that he didn't want to be with anyone because he had major commitment issues to overcome. So yes I know I said sometimes you're the problem, but if you're in a dead-end relationship, he's the problem (or rather, the relationship as a whole is a problem) and your best bet is to just move on.

5. Everyone Makes Mistakes

When I talk about mistakes women make in relationships, a lot of women will get hyper defensive and say I'm blaming them and it's not their fault because all men are jerks. That's one way to look at things, but it's not a very productive, helpful way to look at things.

The fact is we all need to understand how relationships work: the dynamics at play, what sets the foundation for an amazing relationship, why some last, and why others don't. It requires being open to the idea that you may be doing things wrong, and that's OK! The biggest relationship mistake that I see being committed, and I was once a major offender, is being too needy and expecting way too much out of a man and a relationship.

No relationship will give you everything. You need to realize fulfillment comes from you, and it precedes being in a relationship. You can't expect a relationship to make you happy, especially when you have no idea how to find happiness on your own,

6. Self-Love Is Everything

What keeps us in bad relationships isn't that all men are jerks or that relationships are so hard or that we're unworthy or that all the good guys are taken. What keeps us in bad relationships is low self-esteem. When you don't value yourself, you will accept and even welcome people who don't value you into your life. You won't see how wrong this is, how unacceptable this is. If you treat yourself badly, you will accept bad treatment from others. Self-love always comes before healthy romantic love.

I never quite realized this one. Instead I had it backwards, I thought once I found a man to love me, then I too would love myself. But I chased after emotionally unavailable damage cases who, of course, were incapable of giving me love. And even if they had been able to give me love, I wouldn't have been able to receive it because I didn't love myself. The subconscious is always looking to prove itself right. If deep down you feel unlovable, then you will go after men who can't love you. Like attracts like. This is key! If you want someone emotionally stable and healthy, someone who is confident and can give and receive love freely, then you also need to be that kind of person. Whether you're single or in a relationship, you have to always focus on being your best possible self.

7. The Chase Is Nonsense!

OK, not total nonsense, it does kind of work. But it isn't sustainable! The chase creates the illusion of confidence and leaves enough uncertainty to create the illusion of chemistry. Everything feels more dramatic and exciting when we don't know how the other person feels. But a relationship isn't built on uncertainty. Yes, that can galvanize things, it can rouse interest, but you need something real in order for that interest to remain and deepen.

I used to be a master at the chase. I could easily lure a guy in and spark his interest, but I could never keep it. And I never understood why. The reason, I believe, is that in the beginning I would always hold myself back just a bit. I would start off a little scared (probably because the boy before had burned me) and that came across as being coy.

Men are the opposite. In the beginning they usually come on full force. They see an opportunity and they want to grab it. This begins as the perfect combination; he gets to pursue with all his might, and she makes it a little tough. But eventually she (or me) will give in, will get excited, will make it easier on him because she likes him. But if she isn't coming from the right place, if she's a little insecure and needy, if she craves his validation and approval, if she makes it all about him...then he's gone.

This is why the chase doesn't work. Real relationships require being real, being present, being vulnerable. And they demand that both people be in good places emotionally, otherwise things will quickly unravel or become toxic.

8. Men & Women Fall In Love Differently

They also need different things in a relationship. Men primarily need to feel appreciated for who they are and what they have to give. He needs to feel like a winner. If he doesn't, then he won't want to be in the relationship for very long. You'll notice in most breakups and divorces that the guy says the reason it ended is he no longer felt appreciated, he felt like he couldn't make her happy, like she was always harping on him about something. Men need to feel like the man, they need to be respected for what they provide (this does not only mean material items). Find any man who is unhappy in his relationship and ask him why, and his answer will fall under the umbrella of this concept every time.

9. Men Lose Interest For Reasons You Can't See...

There are overt behaviors that push men away, and there are covert ones...the latter causing a lot more confusion than the former! A few months before I started dating my husband I dated a guy I'll call Aaron. We met at a party and instantly hit it off. He was sexy, successful, cool, charming, and absolutely crazy about me. I resisted his advances in the beginning, feeling a little unsure about things because he was two years younger than I was and seemed to still be living like a college kid in a lot of ways, but eventually I stopped analyzing and started to just enjoy. We texted endlessly, went on a few fun dates, and then it hit me...this might really be something!

Then I started to obsess. But what about the fact that he loves to party so much? Can I handle that even though I'm over that phase of my life? And does that mean he won't be ready for marriage? And he's kind of immature...can I live with that? And how will it work between us...our backgrounds are so different. I was busy plugging away mentally, trying to make this relationship work—I was ready to fight for it.

Then we went on another date. I was a little anxious, a little uneasy, and something just changed dramatically. Even though we shared a passionate kiss at the end of the date I knew I wouldn't be hearing from him again. And I was right. And I was also baffled.

What went wrong? Well, my vibe had totally changed and it squeezed the life out of the relationship...and it wasn't even an actual relationship yet. It's not totally my fault, the relationship clearly wasn't meant to last, but it still hurt that he could so quickly lose interest when he'd come on so strong at first. Stressing over a relationship usually ruins it. As does getting attached to a certain outcome. When you expect a serious relationship to unfold with a guy you're casually dating, then you lose something if the relationship ends. When you can just go with it, you only have something to gain.

10. It Doesn't Matter What You Say, It's The Way You Say It

I used to be a terrible communicator. No, scratch that. I was able to effectively communicate in certain settings. My direct, no-nonsense, intellectually thought-out and unemotional way of speaking served me well in terms of my career, but it didn't do me many favors when it came to my relationships.

Communication is a huge determining factor in whether a relationship will survive or fail. You have to learn how to speak in a way so the other person hears you, otherwise you're just wasting your breath and getting nowhere.

You can still make your point, but try to do it from a place of compassion and empathy.

Endnotes

1 Howe, L.C. and Dweck, C.S. (2015) "Changes in self-definition impede recovery from rejection," Personality and Social Psychology Bulletin, 42(1), pp. 54–71. Available at: https://doi.org/10.1177/0146167215612743.

2 The Sainsbury's Living Well Index (no date). Available at: https://about.sainsburys.co.uk/~/media/Files/S/Sainsburys/living-well-index/sainsburys-living-well-index-may-2018.pdf (Accessed: October 26, 2022).

Sabrina Alexis Bendory is the co-founder and co-editor of A New Mode, a website created to help people understand relationship dynamics and how to get the love they want. She has a degree in psychology and has spent over a decade interviewing countless men to understand human psychology and how men operate.

sabrinabendory.com
thoughtcatalog.com/sabrina-bendory
tiktok.com/@sabrinabendory

Other THOUGHT CATALOG titles
published by AMARYLLIS in India

THE PIVOT YEAR

THE MOUNTAIN IS YOU

WHEN YOU'RE READY THIS IS HOW YOU HEAL

101 ESSAYS THAT WILL CHANGE THE WAY YOU THINK

CEREMONY

THIS WAS MEANT TO FIND YOU:
WHEN YOU NEEDED IT MOST

THIS IS ME LETTING YOU GO

SALT WATER

EVERYTHING YOU'LL EVER NEED
YOU CAN FIND WITHIN YOURSELF

THE HUMAN ELEMENT

THE STRENGTH IN OUR SCARS

THE TRUTH ABOUT EVERYTHING

ALL THE WORDS I SHOULD HAVE SAID

BEAUTY IN THE STILLNESS